Take The FEAR Out Of ASKING For Major Gifts

James A. DONOVAN

www.donovanmanagement.com

Dedication

*This book is dedicated to the memory of
my father and mother*
James H. and Esther R. Donovan
*who taught me that a generous spirit
is wealth enough for this life.*

Copyright 2008 by James A. Donovan

Revised Edition, 2008
First Edition, 1993

Donovan Management, Inc.
www.donovanmanagement.com
P.O. Box 471438
Lake Monroe, FL 32747-1438

Printed in the United States of America

All Rights Reserved.

No portion of this book may be reproduced without written permission from the author.

ISBN 0-9639875-1-8

Table of Contents

Forward i
Preface ii
Acknowledgements vi
Looking Back / Looking Forward vii
My Initiation 1

Part I
How to Prepare Before You Ask 3
    Points of Differentiation 3
    Points of Differentiation Ranked From Most
      to Least Important to the Prospect 4
    Who Gives What to Whom 6
    Why People Give 9
    Six Reasons Why People Don't Give 13
    Four Common Fears in Asking for Major Gifts 17
    Knowledge Overcomes Fear 18
    Consider the Prospect's Needs 23
    Who are the Best Prospects 25
    A Typical Gift Table $1,000,000 27
    Summary of Part I 28

Part II
Where To Begin 33
    How to Solicit Your Board or Campaign Committee 36
    How Do We Find Potential Donors 38
    How Do We Rate/Evaluate Prospects 39
    Sample Job Description for Prospect Researcher 44
    Summary of Part II 46

Table of Contents
Continued

Part III
The Asking Process: The APOC Method 49
- Preparation 50
- The Appointment 53
- Strategy 54
- The APOC Method 56
- Case Statement Exercise 65
- Summary of Part III 71

Part IV
Dealing with Objections 75
- Five Steps to Handling Objections 76
- Summary of Part IV 81

Part V
How to Close the Major Gift 87
- The No/Yes Close 87
- The Investment Close 88
- The Ego Close 89
- The Double-It Tactic 90
- Follow-Up 92
- Summary of Part V 94

A Checklist of Reminders 95

Frequently Asked Questions 97

A Final Word 110

Exhibits 111
- Sample Personal Proposal Document 111
- Sample Talking Points 121
- Best Practice Tips 122

Forward
William L. Carlton, ACFRE

This book was a breakthrough in 1993 and continues with this new edition. It is a great updating and refinement of helpful techniques required for successful major gift solicitations.

Far beyond an academic exercise, Mr. Donovan and I have road tested this approach throughout the United States in Association of Fund Raising Professionals (AFP) Chapter meetings and more importantly in numerous client settings with volunteer leadership. The book is terrific. Seeing Jim Donovan teach these principles in person is even better. He's passionate about motivating people to overcome their fear of asking.

Volunteers, especially in recent years, are less comfortable in asking for major gifts. Moreover, many who would like to get involved often do not because of their fear and dislike of fund raising. *Take the Fear Out of Asking for Major Gifts* is a helpful resource with step by step guidance in what Jim Donovan calls the art of "invitation".

More importantly, Mr. Donovan's approach is faithful to the essence of philanthropy—personal voluntary actions in support of the common good. True philanthropy begins with the "heart" and this new edition will enable the volunteer to use both the heart and the mind to advance important programs and projects for a better world. Helpful for the professional and volunteer alike, this new edition is a welcomed overhaul to an already seminal work in the field.

It is a pleasure for me to introduce this new edition. I plan to use this book consistently, as previously, in helping our clients, particularly their leadership volunteers, in asking without fear.

William L. Carlton, ACFRE
Chairman, Carlton and Company
Boston, MA

Mr. Carlton serves as chairman of the ACFRE Certification Board and is a member of the AFP National Board of Directors

Preface

"It doesn't hurt to ask." How many times have friends, family, and colleagues given this sage advice to us when we were confronted with the anxiety of asking for a small favor, such as directions when trying to locate a particular street address or when trying to find out if a particular company is hiring or not? We have all been motivated at one time or another by this adage to charge ahead. Not to worry – "The only thing they can say is 'no'."

Having spent my entire professional career in the nonprofit sector, I recall how often I have heard professional colleagues and volunteers of nonprofit institutions use this pearl of wisdom as their motivation for soliciting a major gift prospect. Over the years this has struck me as a negative motivator. It's sort of like the famous quote attributed to the notorious gangster, Al Capone. He was reported to have said, "You can get more with a kind word and a gun than you can with just a kind word."

When I started my consulting practice, I found myself spending a lot of time training clients' volunteers on how to make a proper solicitation for a major gift. The training sessions included a wide range of individuals who invariably approached their task of making assigned solicitations with great anxiety. As these training seminars got underway, some people would actually get up and leave. As they exited the room, they would say, "I'm sorry, but I just can't do this. I'm just not comfortable. I'm too afraid the prospect will say 'no'." Even those volunteers who made a living in sales or who were members of the institution's board of directors had a degree of fear when it came to soliciting a major gift. I suddenly realized that one of the services that my clients desperately needed was training that would take the fear out of asking for the major gift they were assigned or had volunteered to solicit.

The fear of asking, in my judgement, is one of the main reasons for the noticeable shift in responsibility for major gift solicitation from the traditional volunteer/peer level to the professional staff. A disturbing trend to say the least. **Anyone who has been associated with professional fund raising knows that there is no substitute for a high-powered volunteer soliciting one of his/her own peers.** This is not to say that the professional staff should be left out of the process. Obviously not. There is a place for both the volunteer and the staff member, and the two combined, in my experience, make the best solicitation team. Nonprofit institutions need to get back to this basic tenet of fund raising if they are to succeed in the highly competitive market of charitable giving.

Franklin D. Roosevelt said it best, "We have nothing to fear but fear itself." Fear is a paralyzer for many people. Take, for example, those folks who are afraid to fly. Some are afraid of heights. Others do not like the lack of control of the aircraft. Many feel too confined in the close quarters of the airplane. Most don't like the idea of not being able to see the "road" up ahead. Whatever the reasons, these people avoid flying because they are filled with fear.

Those who have the courage to face their fears try to overcome them by enrolling in special seminars with others who are equally scared of flying. They put themselves in the hands of professional psychologists and airline safety experts who address their fears. Very often, their therapy starts with just showing up at the airport. Then approaching the door of the aircraft.

Every step is slow and gradual until eventually they take off on a real flight. The success of this anxiety-reducing program is built upon one key component – knowledge. People are given information that reinforces the safety of air travel. The focus is not on what can go wrong when flying, but on the many systems and back-up systems that are responsible for air travel being so safe today.

Like the fearful flyer, there are thousands of fearful volunteers today who believe in their cause, are willing to donate thousands of volunteer service hours to advance the cause, but refuse to "ask for money" because they are afraid. They fear rejection, embarrassment, and in some cases, even reciprocity – a donor turning around and asking for a contribution to **his or her** favorite charity. Having a cadre of dedicated volunteers is a blessing to any nonprofit institution. **However, it can be very frustrating to a professional fund raiser when these volunteers agree to do anything but ask for money.**

That's why I have written this book. To assist these legions of volunteers associated with thousands of nonprofit institutions across the United States and abroad to become more comfortable and confident in asking for major gifts. This book is the outgrowth of a training program I developed over a period of seven years. It has been presented dozens of times to volunteer and professional fund raising groups from Orlando to Oregon as **Take the Fear**

Out of Asking For Major Gifts. Fortunately, it has struck a responsive and timely chord as my audiences encouraged me to expand the seminar into a book.

In the many years that I have been presenting the live seminar, I, too, have learned from the seminar participants, particularly from their questions. Their concerns were a guide to me in continually refining the seminar and knowing what subjects needed more elaboration or clarification. This listening to the audience resulted in placing more emphasis in this book on dealing with the prospect's objections, explaining the case for support, and even how to get the appointment with the prospect in the first place. Each of these topics is now covered in greater detail than in the live seminar.

If an instructor does his job right, he can learn as much from his students as his students learn from him. I am deeply indebted to the thousands of seminar attendees who have helped me understand their fears and concerns in the asking of major gifts. What they taught me is included in the pages that follow. After seven years of presenting, listening, and refining, I am confident that this book reflects what seminar participants have "asked" for.

Whether you're a veteran or novice volunteer or staff member of a nonprofit institution, it is my hope that you find this book the most concise, clear, and helpful publication today on this subject of fear and major gifts fund raising. That certainly was my goal in writing it and now in updating it.

THIS BOOK WILL SHOW YOU HOW TO:

Target your markets

Present your case for support

Ask for major gifts effectively

Overcome objections from prospects

Make yourself more comfortable and confident
in asking for major gifts

Acknowledgements

I am especially grateful to:

- My wife Janet, for her many hours in converting the book's original text in a format that allowed me to edit it, for her proofing this revised edition and encouraging me to "get it done." Thank you, Dear.

- Mary Harowski, a former client and part-time Communications Specialist for Donovan Management, who is a joy to work with.

- Bill Carlton, a personal and professional friend of over twenty plus years, who reviewed the first edition and now has written a most gracious **Forward** for this revised edition.

- The **Council on Aging of Martin County, Florida** for allowing me to use the **Talking Points Card** I devised for them for their capital campaign.

- The **Association of Fundraising Professionals** for permission to use the *Donor Bill of Rights*.

- My golden retrievers, **Cobey** and **Reilly**, and my daughter's golden retriever **Cayman** (whom we doggie day care) for nudging my arm after hours at the computer to remind me it was time for a break, actually play time for them.

- Finally to the thousands of professional staff and volunteers who allowed me to teach the principles of this book to them in seminars, workshops and retreats over the years. Your questions, comments and insights were the inspiration to update this edition. I hope I have given back as much as you have given me.

James A. Donovan

From the Author
Looking Back/Looking Forward

This book was first published in 1993. In the ensuing years it has been most gratifying to see how many volunteers and fund raising professionals in the United States, the Caribbean and many European countries have benefited from it. Equally satisfying is the wide range of nonprofit organizations that have purchased this book, including many professionals of the nation's largest and most prestigious colleges, universities and medical centers. However, there is no substitute for being at a conference where someone seeks me out to tell me their personal story of how the book made the difference in obtaining a major gift.

Readers have told me over and over again, they love the book's title, *"Take the Fear Out of Asking for Major Gifts."* I guess in the early nineties there was no shortage of volunteers that dreaded asking someone for money so it appears now that I was on to something. It's hard to imagine professional (paid) staff being timid about asking for major gifts but there were a fair number of them who assured me the book helped them overcome their fears.

In looking back at the time this book was first published in 1993 the Internet was just starting to be used by development professionals. Sophisticated prospect screening and advanced methods of prospect research were non-existent online. Many professionals kept computer files and reports on major donors and prospects in written documents, unlike today's complex computerized donor record keeping systems that have spawned dozens of firms catering to fund raising research staff.

Back then few development offices had a dedicated staff person whose sole function was researching major gift prospects. Today, there are hundreds of professionals doing this work. It has even resulted in a whole new association of professionals who make their living searching for wealth indicators, donors giving to similar charities and a prospect's social connections. Today the *Association of Professional Researchers for Advancement* has a growing membership that performs tasks under a strict code-of-ethics, provides on-going education seminars/conferences and special resources to its members.

Those development offices that cannot afford an in-house prospect researcher have assigned these tasks to existing staff that, thanks to technology today, multi-task in their search for information. Staff will do their own Google search, spend countless hours of clicking a trail to find that one gem of information that can make the difference in the ask for a major gift. But, beware of what I call the *paralysis of analysis*. What good is all the intelligence if the ask is never made?

In the past when using this book for staff and volunteer training or in giving seminars for the *Association of Fundraising Professionals* and other groups, I would always talk about the *solicitation* of major gifts. That it was the job of professional staff and leadership volunteers to get out there and solicit. Today I now substitute the word *solicitation* with *invitation*, because that's really what major gift fund raisers and volunteers do – *invite* others to become a part of a noble enterprise such as wiping out cancer in our lifetime, preventing forest fires, saving the whales, not wasting a mind.

Just consider the connotation of the word solicitation. What images does it conjure up? Being solicited at the dinner hour by a telemarketer or having a fireman's boot shoved in your face at a traffic light or even a homeless person working a street corner. On the other hand, the word *invitation* makes you feel special. You've been selected, identified, sought out as having the qualities that are socially endearing. You are special. Being *invited* to give implies not just anyone is welcome or needed in the particular enterprise being promoted.

This concept of invitation vs. solicitation really hit me in the late nineties when working with the Puerto Rico Chapter of the American Red Cross. We were doing a major gifts campaign for the Chapter's 100th Anniversary. The Spanish culture there is obviously the dominant culture so the typical approach taken in the States wasn't going to work. There wasn't going to be a "Clara Barton Society" in Puerto Rico.

So I had to come up with something that would hit home, literally. As luck would have it, as part of the anniversary celebration, a special lecture was given by a local/distinguished professor on the one-hundred year history of the Red Cross movement on the island, which had its origins in Spain. It turned out that three individuals – a doctor, a nurse and a highly regarded government official – provided key leadership during the century long span. Each in his/her own way built on the success of others. Thus, we created the *Honor Society of the American Red Cross of Puerto Rico* with three levels of membership each named after one of the movement's pioneers. Those three names resonated with the target audience as many citizens of Puerto Rico could trace their family history to one of them. Overnight, the Honor Society had the perception and feel of an exclusive club that one could not join but had to be *invited* into.

Only weeks into the program the development director of the Red Cross along with a board member (who had already signed on as an Honor Society member) called on a prospect, a successful businessman. When they arrived at his office, he overheard his assistant greet them and he immediately came out of his office and instructed her to whisk them in and then proceeded to tell her, "These are Red Cross leaders and they have come to my office today to *invite me* to become a member of a very special organization that advances the work of the Red Cross here on the island."

My client reported back to me this gentleman was worried he wouldn't get in the club. I knew then for that culture "the ask" had to be about *invitation not solicitation.* So I thought to myself, why just in Puerto Rico, why not everywhere? What has confirmed this strategic shift for me is the reaction I have gotten since then from the thousands of persons in seminars I have conducted with my new emphasis on invitation. It was as if a thousand light bulbs went off. The facial expression alone did it for me. Then the comments during the break, "Gee, it makes all the sense in the world."

Another important factor in looking forward is the need for honing one's communications skills. When growing up as a kid in Central New York we had but one television station, an NBC affiliate. My younger brother and sister grew up with the addition of ABC as well as cable television being added to our household. Today, there are dozens of cable and network channels devoted to news around the clock. Satellite television makes the options endless. The one constant of all this change is the traditional thirty, sixty or ninety second television advertisement. Millions of mini-sound bites each day touting the benefits of all day deodorants, tooth whitening products or online mortgages.

Add to this the hundreds of emails and instant email messages, online pop-up ads, billboards, recorded telephone sales pitches, voice mail messages, Palm Pilot/Blackberry messages -- you become a giant message absorbing sponge. So you tune-out rather than tune-in the messages. **Today the challenge for fund raisers seeking major gifts has more to do with communication than cultivation or invitation.** One must be able to get his point across in two minutes or less, thus, the necessity for the fund raiser's two minute elevator speech.

To fine tune your elevator speech, listen to others give their version, be it a political lobbyist, life insurance salesperson or the Girl Scout selling boxes of cookies at your door.

Having said this, don't get me wrong. I am not advocating that you reduce an all important ask for a major gift to a two minute pitch. What I am suggesting is that you do your best to give the highlights of your case in two minutes or less. After doing so engage the prospect in a meaningful dialogue. This isn't an easy exercise. It takes practice. Those who make the effort see an improvement in the number of major gifts they obtain. The elevator speech answers four key questions for the prospect as noted in Part III.

The greatest impediment today to being a successful major gifts fund raiser is the constant flow of email and voicemail making the live telephone conversation an anomaly. Technology has become the Velcro that binds you to your desk, keeping you from the important task at hand, getting face to face with the major gift prospects. If there was ever a time to listen to the sage advice of the greatest management consultant of our time, Peter F. Drucker, it's now. *"It's not important to get things done, it's important to get the right things done."* Stephen Covey says the same thing when he reminds us to distinguish between what is urgent and important and what is simply urgent.

The essence of major gift fund raising is relationships -- cultivating them, nurturing them, maintaining them. As a consultant who has done thousands of capital campaign study interviews with current and prospective major gift prospects and donors, I hear first hand how donors made major gifts, were thanked, then no more contact, as if the donor had contracted a highly contagious disease. The truth is fund raising professionals do change jobs, too often and too soon, leaving behind too little information on the donor for the next professional. Staff does come and go but the institution lives on. So too do their donors.

The road ahead for major gift fund raising is exciting when one considers that by the year 2016 we will probably see a record $600 billion in giving in the United States.

When I started my career I thought raising a million dollars for the United Way of Utica, New York was a milestone. A million dollars? Decades later, in 2006, I was stunned like the rest of us when Warren Buffet rocked the philanthropy world by announcing his plan to give over $30 billion to the *Bill & Melinda Gates Foundation* in Seattle, Washington.

I believe the best is yet to be. Globalization, like the high-tech boom of the nineties, is adding a whole new crop of wealthy entrepreneurs who will take advantage of gifting to charity appreciated stock of their own company. Baby boomers will inherit millions. Each will want to leave behind a legacy of generosity. I hope this book inspires you to invite without fear the *uninvited* billions of dollars there for the asking.

Who Gives?
Sources of Contributions

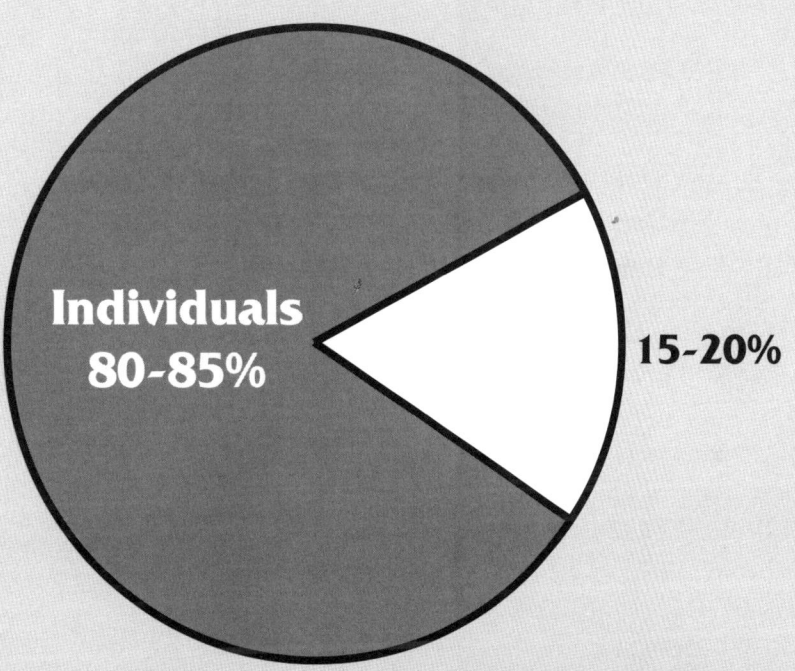

Historically, individuals have given 80-85% of all contributions year after year according to the Giving Institute, "Giving USA Report". The remaining 15-20% comes from corporations, foundations, special groups and other sources. Giving in 2006 was just under $300 million, according to the Institute.

THE BOOK CONSISTS OF FIVE PARTS

I. How to Prepare Before You Ask
II. Where Do I Begin
III. The Asking Process: The APOC Method
IV. Dealing with Objections: The APOC Method Continued
V. How to Close the Major Gift

My Initiation

The purpose of this book is to provide you with a better understanding of how to prepare yourself in asking for major gifts. **I define a major gift as a cash, securities or deferred gift of $10,000 or more.** Asking for a gift of this size requires advance preparation. Those who have been successful in obtaining major gifts know preparation is the secret to success. Major gift solicitation is a serious enterprise requiring thorough homework before "the ask" is made.

This book is based upon an observation I made years ago: People are basically afraid to ask for money. They fear even the **thought** of asking someone to give to their favorite charity. Therefore, taking the fear out of asking is a critical objective of this book.

Early in my career, especially during my first job with the United Way, I learned that there were two kinds of successful solicitors. Those with clout who were not afraid to ask those prospects who seemed to be subject to their influence, and those who were often at least on a par with the prospect. Clearly, fewer solicitors who have that kind of clout are assisting nonprofit campaigns today. Those kinds of solicitors are being replaced with legions of caring, cause-minded solicitors, who are bold in their beliefs, but shy when it comes to asking for a major gift. These staff members and volunteers approach their task of solicitation like a politician giving a faint-hearted endorsement on an issue. They say what they have to say for the record, but do so with little passion.

I recall one United Way Campaign volunteer who was a State Farm insurance agent. Every time we had a committee meeting, he found himself giving a sales lesson to the other volunteers. He would espouse the same techniques he used in selling State Farm insurance policies to prospects, making his case that these same techniques could be used to sell people on making a special ($5,000) pledge to the United Way campaign.* He was a successful agent with a very polished approach. The problem was that the other volunteers were not buying it. They felt there was a difference between selling insurance and "selling" the United Way. It took me a while to figure out the group's underlying fear. During the third committee meeting, it surfaced.

*5,000 at that time was considered a significant gift.

A woman in the group spoke up and said, "John, when you sell your customers on State Farm, you give them a tangible return for their investment. My fear in all of this is trying to convince a donor what's tangible about making a $5,000 gift to the United Way." The State Farm agent wasn't able to address her concerns. He really didn't know how to.

Being the newest member of the staff, I turned to the veterans present hoping they would chime in with an answer. The suggestions ranged from, "Tell them this is the United Way and it's the right thing to do for their community" to "We have an obligation to help the less fortunate." None of the suggestions provided the confident answer that the solicitor needed to overcome her fear. I started to wonder what kind of profession I had gotten myself into – selling an intangible!

Back then, we failed to come up with the right answer. Shortly after this incident, I discovered the answer. **Real generosity had to start in the heart, not in the mind. It was an emotional reaction driven by a desire to feel good.** To overcome this fear of selling the intangible, solicitors had to be taught to encourage people to think of their giving as being a part of something bigger than themselves. In other words, a cause or movement which helps people and makes a difference in their lives.

I believe the best illustration of this concept is the United Jewish Appeal (UJA). When prospects are solicited for the UJA, they are encouraged to put the needs of the entire State of Israel and the local Jewish Community Center ahead of their own individual need for a tangible return. Modern day fund raising owes much to the lessons learned from the way the UJA conducts its solicitations.

The State Farm experience was my initiation to what has turned out to be a career pursuit of asking, learning and teaching what I believe are sound principles of major gift fund raising.

A Word Of Caution

Most states now require some form of registration before the solicitation of contributions can begin on behalf of a nonprofit organization. This varies from state to state as do the requirements for volunteer, staff and consultant registration. Before beginning your major gifts program, be sure to check with your state department of consumer affairs.

***Never measure your generosity
by what you give,
but rather by what
you have left.***

- Archbishop Fulton J. Sheen

Part I.

HOW TO PREPARE BEFORE YOU ASK

The first step in preparing for the solicitation of any major gift is to take inventory of the unique characteristics that *differentiate* your organization, institution, or agency from others. A common complaint we consultants hear from prospective donors is, "These charities are all the same." Thus, you have to ask yourself, "What are the differentiating factors of your institution?"

For example, if you are seeking a major gift from a prospect for a new public library, you might list some of these factors that differentiate your library from others in the region.

POINTS OF DIFFERENTIATION

1. User friendly computer stations for the elderly
2. Support staff to help users navigate the worldwide web
3. A children's section with safeguards from online predators
4. Open longer on weekends to accommodate business owners
5. A quiet atmosphere thanks to noise suppression technology

Now prioritize these points according to the point of view of the prospect you are approaching, in this case let's say, a local business owner. List them from most to least important to the prospect. For example:

POINTS OF DIFFERENTIATION RANKED FROM MOST TO LEAST IMPORTANT TO THE PROSPECT

1. Open longer on weekends to accommodate business owners
2. A children's section with safeguards from online predators
3. User friendly computer stations for the elderly
4. A quiet atmosphere thanks to noise suppression technology
5. Support staff to help users navigate the worldwide web

Each factor must be carefully considered by fully understanding the climate in the community. The best source of determining this climate is the library staff itself. They know firsthand about the demand for new and better services. Other user groups may include the Friends of the Library, cardholders, local educators and business people in the community. After talking with each of these groups, add any new items to the list and prioritize the list from the most to least important factors based on your discussions with them.

Test this final list by talking with three or four other groups such as members or staff at the local Chamber of Commerce, bankers, and professionals such as accountants, lawyers, and medical personnel, to obtain their reactions. Use their reactions and suggestions to refine your final list. You now have the most salient sales points according to the consumer and constituent groups you will be approaching for contributions.

Knowing what you have to sell is vital. Emphasizing your institution's uniqueness is absolutely essential. There are over one million nonprofit groups in the United States. Many have similar missions and compete in the same communities. What makes your nonprofit different and more worthy of support? Be sure you have the answer to this question before you begin asking for major gifts.

Take a few minutes now and complete the exercise as shown on the next page. Begin by listing all the sales points you can think of as they come to mind. Then go back, prioritize them and fill in the form provided. Keep these in mind as they will be very important in preparing your case for support, which is discussed later.

Exercise

Characteristics of your Organization

Using Key Words, List Sales Points Below:

1. _____ 5. _____

2. _____ 6. _____

3. _____ 7. _____

4. _____ 8. _____

Divide Them Into Most and Least Important Categories

Most Important	Least Important

© James A. Donovan

WHO GIVES WHAT TO WHOM

The next step in preparing for the solicitation of a major gift is recognizing some important facts and statistics on who gives what to whom. The nation's leading trade group that tracks such trends is the *Giving Institute*, formerly the *American Association of Fund Raising Counsel* (AAFRC). Each year it publishes Giving USA, a report on overall giving patterns in the country. You may obtain a copy of this publication by calling, writing or emailing them at: www.aafrc.org. You should take time to read this report as well as periodicals and newspapers that cover the field of fund raising. Another good source for giving trends is the Chronicle of Philanthropy at: www.philanthropy.com which also has its annual Philanthropy 400, a ranking of nonprofits by income.

One statistic, as noted earlier, that astonishes volunteer solicitors and staff alike is the fact that over eighty percent of all giving in the United States is from individuals. This is a statistic that you should use in focusing yourself and your solicitors on the right prospect pool - **individuals** rather than corporations or foundations.

Giving in 2006 in the United States reached $295.02 billion, according to the *Giving USA Report* by the *Giving Institute.* Of this amount, 75.6% or $222.89 billion came from individuals. When you combine this total with bequests also made by individuals, the percentage of the total is an astounding 83.4% or $245.80 billion. Generally speaking, giving in the U.S. doubles every ten years. If this trend continues, total giving in the U.S. could exceed $600 billion by the year 2016.

I often begin addressing a volunteer board with the question, "Out of the hundreds of billions given in the U.S. last year, what percent would you say was given by foundations and corporations combined?" Invariably, the answer given is 50%. Having read these reports for over thirty years now, the one constant is the overwhelming fact that year after year about three-quarters of all giving is from individuals. Foundations in 2006 gave 12.4% or $36.5 billion. Corporations gave 4.3% or $12.7 billion. These facts are critical in your fund raising strategy for major gifts. Imagine if your board believed that corporations and foundations would be the source of the majority of your major gifts. Remember, in the end, individuals enable you to meet your major gift fund raising goals.

It's also important to note the recipient of these donated billions. In years past, religious groups consistently received the largest percentage of all giving. In 2006, they received 32.8% or just under $100 billion ($96 billion) of the $295 total. Clearly, the most prevalent factor in motivating individuals to give is religious belief. It's important to point out that funds earmarked for religion also provide assistance to the needy. Most religious congregations make grants to social service agencies throughout the year as part of their outreach programs. Thus, not all funds to religion are for the operation of houses of worship and church-related activities.

To better understand the environment in which major gifts are solicited today, it's helpful to observe some societal trends.

For example, as noted earlier, the $30 billion Warren Buffet gift to the Gates Foundation. In the mid-nineties a gift that made similar headlines was that of Ambassador Walter H. Annenberg when he contributed $355 million to four educational institutions. Gifts of $100 million or more are becoming commonplace in many hospital and higher-education campaigns. This pattern is expected to continue as more amass their fortunes in a global economy.

Corporate mergers and acquisitions have left many majority shareholders wealthy beyond their wildest dreams. They are also a likely source of such mega-gifts.

State lotteries have created hundreds of new millionaires in lottery states. Multi-state Powerball lotteries that pay out $100 million or more to a single winner are becoming common.

The Microsoft company, founded by William Gates, has generated 2,200 millionaires due to the growth in that company's stock. The founders of Google and other online search engine companies have amassed fortunes that make the Rockefeller and Carnegie wealth appear minimal.

In the strategic planning for many major campaigns, emphasis is being centered on a fifty-percent lead gift: one donor agrees to a mega-gift with the understanding that an equal amount will be raised in a broad-based public campaign. If a mega-gift isn't feasible many campaigns today are being floored with a gift that represents twenty percent of the campaign goal. Recently I had the opportunity to conduct solicitor training for a capital campaign team that was the client of another firm out of the northeast. The donor agreed to fund one-half of the campaign goal but restricted his gift to an endowment for the operation and upkeep of the new museum when completed. Not only did the campaign get a huge head start, it instantly overcame one of the major objections of foundation executives and other donors regarding how the organization was going to keep the facility operating once built. Needless to say the campaign exceeded its goal in short order.

The pressure on the wealthy to share their good fortune with the less fortunate will continue to build as the gap between the rich and poor continues to grow.

Everyday the news media carries reports about more and more Americans becoming wealthy, especially professional athletes, musicians, singers, actors, and actresses. Admittedly, many of them establish their own private foundations for what appeals to their sense of philanthropy, but the fact remains that many of them are good prospects for a local major gift campaign.

From time to time Congress passes new legislation raising or lowering taxes. In August of 2006 President Bush signed into law the **Pension Protection Act**. This Act allowed taxpayers/donors to direct charitable transfers from their **Individual Retirement Accounts**. If a donor/ couple is 70.5 years of age or older, he/she may be eligible to transfer up to $100,000 each, $200,000 total per couple, to charity from their IRA per year in 2006 and 2007.

When Congress lowers the tax rate, it costs donors more of their own money when giving. If Congress raises taxes, it costs the donor less. For example, when the top rate was 50 percent, Uncle Sam was paying one-half of the total cost of a gift. **However, history shows that tax savings are not a motivation for giving, but rather an added benefit for being generous to a charitable cause.**

WHY PEOPLE GIVE

Paul H. Schneiter, in his book **The Art of Asking** (1978, Walker and Company, New York), has listed many commonly known reasons why people give to nonprofit organizations. These are:

1. Religious beliefs
2. Self-preservation
3. Guilt
4. Tax savings
5. Obligation
6. Recognition
7. Pressure

As already noted, religious beliefs rank as the number one motivation for giving. Scripture tells us of the importance of tithing. The Protestant denominations, historically, have done an excellent job in encouraging their congregations to tithe. Catholics, however, are not nearly as effective in tithing, but they have made progress in the last ten years by implementing stewardship programs that embrace the concept of tithing. Jewish synagogues and related causes, such as the United Jewish Appeal, are extremely successful at fund raising. When it comes to giving, the religiously active set the pace and have strong convictions based upon biblical exhortations for doing so.

The second reason people give is out of a sense of self-preservation and fear. In the first edition of this book I gave the example of the AIDS epidemic. Unless a cure is found for this killer disease, millions of people may die. The government estimates that it will cost several billions of dollars before a cure is discovered.

Environmental groups have made great strides in recent years by raising public awareness of the implications of global warming on our fragile planet.

Who doesn't fear a diagnosis of cancer? The American Cancer Society

Seven Reasons People Give

1. Religious beliefs
2. Self-preservation
3. Guilt
4. Tax savings
5. Obligation
6. Recognition
7. Pressure

Source: The Art of Asking, Paul H. Schneiter, 1978, Walker and Company, New York

tells its donors and prospects, "We want to wipe out cancer in your lifetime." That appeals to a person's sense of self-preservation.

"Extinction Is Forever" is a great theme for preserving wildlife such as whales, panda bears, and the American bald eagle. In this case, people link self-preservation with the preservation of other species.

Self-preservation and the fear of not surviving clearly come into play when making decisions to give to a health-related cause.

The third reason people give is out of a sense of guilt. Often times, people feel they have neglected doing their fair share for others, so they try to make up for it by contributing to a charity. Shortly after the inner-city turbulence of the 1960's, many corporations contributed heavily to urban reconstruction and housing programs. The south central Los Angeles riots of 1992 motivated one organization to contribute $75 million toward rebuilding the riot-torn area.

The fourth reason for giving is to save money on taxes. This motivation for giving has always been overestimated. As already noted, the tax incentive for giving isn't what it used to be. It actually costs a donor more to give today than in years past. Donors certainly want every deduction they are entitled to; however, saving on taxes is a secondary consideration.

The fifth reason for giving is obligation. College graduates feel obligated to contribute to their alumni fund because they feel indebted to their alma mater for the success they enjoy today. Others have family members who received services from an agency and feel they should help out such an organization. For example, people who have used the services of Hospice often feel obligated to contribute in memory of a loved one in appreciation for the service their family member received.

The sixth reason for giving is recognition. We all enjoy being recognized and publicly thanked for our generosity. Opportunities for donor recognition are prominently discussed in fund raising literature. The most popular form of major gift recognition in any capital campaign is the naming of a new building after the donor. This usually requires a gift covering fifty to one hundred percent of the total cost of the building. Recognition is also provided in the more modest form of an honor roll, which features the names of donors in an institution's annual report.

The seventh reason for giving is pressure. Many a major donor has been pressured to give. A bank president who heads up the campaign for a new community library may pressure a borrower from his bank, such as a major car dealer, to give to the library project. The pressure may be subtle; nevertheless, it becomes clear to major customers that he wants to meet his goal, and a gift would be most welcomed.

As Jerold Panas, author of "MegaGifts", points out, another reason people give is to make a difference in society. This would certainly be the case in the recent $30 billion gift made by Warren Buffet to the Gates Foundation.

Always keep in mind these reasons why people give. Better yet, make sure to anticipate which of these reasons would best motivate each of your major gift prospects.

SIX REASONS WHY PEOPLE DON'T GIVE

Knowing why people **don't** give when asked is equally important as knowing why they do. What you do before and during the process of asking is more important than anything else. The six most important reasons people don't give are as follows:

1. You failed to properly research the prospect before asking for the gift. It's important to know the following about the prospect before you ask for a major gift:
    - prior giving record at your institution
    - prior giving record to other charities
    - any restrictions on their gift
    - payment of gift (was it paid in full?)
    - cumulative giving record
    - who was the last volunteer or staff person to solicit them
    - best time of year to ask
    - other preferences the prospect may have

How you obtain this type of information is discussed in Part II of this book.

2. You failed to ask for a specific amount or in a specific range. I distinctly recall a campaign in which we trained solicitors to ask for a gift of $10,000 from each prospect. Each prospect had been evaluated as having the ability to give at that level. The solicitor assigned to one particular prospect did not ask for that specific amount. In fact, he never mentioned a figure. A week later, we received a check for $100 in the mail from the same prospect who, two years prior, had given over $400,000 to a local university.

Six Reasons Why People Don't Give

People don't give because the fund raiser fails to follow proper procedure in asking for a gift.

1. Failure to do adequate prospect research: premature request.

2. Failure to ask for a specific amount or range of gift levels.

3. Failure to suggest that donor may use multiple resources.

4. Failure to match solicitor to the prospect.

5. Failure to include spouse in the solicitation.

6. Failure to do an adequate follow-up.

© James A. Donovan

I believe it's important to state your minimum request in a range which gives the prospect room to move up or down. In the case above, the solicitor was obviously afraid to mention a specific amount. He and the prospect would have been more comfortable if he had said, "Bill, I was hoping you would consider a gift in the range of $10,000."

3. You failed to suggest to the donor to use multiple resources such as an outright gift of cash or appreciated stock, or a gift of real estate or a combination of an outright gift and an irrevocable gift of life insurance or bequest or a planned gift. Depending on the donor's age, a combination of an outright gift and planned gift might work best depending on the donor's need for income.

4. You or a second member of the solicitation team were not on the same peer level as the prospect. This is not to suggest that you send doctors to solicit doctors and lawyers to solicit lawyers. An owner of the community's largest car dealership may be the best person to approach a wealthy prospect who has his own accounting firm. They belong to the same country club, attend the same church each Sunday, and their daughters are on the same swim team at the local prep school. And, they each have the ability to contribute $10,000 to your campaign. That's a good peer level match up of solicitor and prospect. You must take the time to research these relationships. In doing so, you build success into the solicitation.

5. You excluded the spouse of the prospect when making the request. This happened to me on my own church drive. One Sunday afternoon, I dutifully called upon the five prospects my pastor assigned to me for the church building fund drive. It was my third solicitation of the day and the biggest request that I had planned- $5,000. When I arrived at the prospect's home, the husband answered the door and gave me a warm greeting. I had called ahead of time for the appointment, and he knew exactly why I was

coming. He invited me to sit on the sofa in the living room and proceeded to call his wife, whom I recall was upstairs on the telephone. I engaged in the usual niceties and stalled in the hopes that his wife would soon join us. She came down the stairs and explained to her husband that she had to go pick up her older daughter, who was a few minutes drive from their home, but that she "would be right back."

I continued to talk to the husband, learning that he was in law enforcement. He told me some interesting stories and after about twenty minutes said, "We better get on with this. I know why you are here and my wife and I have been discussing our gift to the church. We've decided to contribute $5,000 payable in the next two years." I thought, "Bingo." I didn't even have to ask. With that response, I handed him the pledge card, had him fill in the amount, sign it and said goodbye. His wife never made it back before I left.

Two weeks later, I learned from my pastor that the donor had lowered the gift to $2,500 over two years, not the $5,000 he had agreed upon. His wife was not pleased that he had committed $5,000 without her participation. I told my pastor what had happened and said, "It was my fault, Father. I should have known better. I should have offered to come back at another time when both husband and wife could be asked together." In the rush to complete my calls, I was anxious to take the husband's pledge. It backfired.

6. You failed to follow up by providing additional information as requested by (and promised to) the prospect. This happens quite often in campaigns where there is a mix of private funding and government funding. Many major gift prospects are suspicious of projects that require two-thirds of the funds in the form of private voluntary contributions with the balance coming from the city, county, state, or federal government. They know that most government dollars can be recalled as easily as they were appropriated.

A prospect may require a copy of the prospectus for the city bond fund, which is earmarking thirty percent of its funds to the new Performing Arts Center. A request like this is quite appropriate to make and requires a quick response. A letter from the city attorney along with a copy of the prospectus (highlighting the section on the certainty of the appropriation) would be an ideal response. Failure to provide this information would, of course, cause the donor to procrastinate and, even worse, assume that your campaign has something to hide.

Now that we have examined the reasons why people give or don't give, the next step in the major gifts process is to analyze the four most common fears that you and other solicitors have in asking for money. **In order to take the fear out of asking, you must first acknowledge and understand the fears that you have when it comes to soliciting.** Most solicitors experience one or more of these fears at some time during a fund raising campaign. Knowing in advance which fears hamper you will allow you to deal with them.

FOUR COMMON FEARS IN ASKING FOR MAJOR GIFTS

- The fear of rejection
- The fear of embarrassment
- The fear of failure
- The fear of mandatory reciprocity

It's perfectly natural to fear rejection. Unless you are a born salesperson, most of us don't handle rejection too well. People who fear rejection believe that it does hurt to ask.

Also, competition for meeting an assigned quota in a campaign is intense. No one wants to be embarrassed at a fund raising meeting by turning in a report that has yielded poor results, especially in front of their peers.

No one wants to be a failure either, especially when he or she is volunteering their precious time for a good cause. It takes a serious commitment of time to properly solicit major gifts. Failure to make this time productive can be most discouraging to you and other solicitors.

Reciprocity comes into play when you know the person you are soliciting will most likely turn right around and ask you for a similar gift to his favorite charity. You solicit a major gift for the Boy Scouts and the prospect says "yes" to your request. Then a few months later, you are asked by this same person to give to the Girl Scouts.

KNOWLEDGE OVERCOMES FEAR

How do you overcome these fears? With knowledge. It's the greatest tool in your major gift toolbox. Knowledge equips the solicitor with an effective blueprint for success. You need to know the answers to the following questions.

ANSWER THE FOLLOWING

- **How to make the case for the institution: Are you selling opportunities instead of needs?**

- **How to ask: What are the key steps in asking?**

- **How to overcome objections: What do you say when they arise?**

- **How to properly solicit: How do you ask for the gift?**

Over the years in which I have made my living as a consultant, I have trained thousands of volunteers in the methods outlined in this book. In each seminar I have given, there is a significant level of anxiety in the room when the seminar begins. I start each seminar by asking participants to mention their own fears in asking. Invariably everyone, even the seasoned veterans, mention some uneasiness in asking for money. I then proceed to inventory their fears. This exercise itself is a confidence builder since it allows the participants to openly admit their lack of confidence, knowing that this is shared by others in the room and it's not something happening just to them. By recognizing these fears, each person can then rationally brainstorm with the group about the information needed to overcome their fears.

I remember one client who had three of the four common fears - rejection, embarrassment and failure. He was a newly appointed Bishop, who found himself inheriting a capital fund drive from the previous Bishop. A feasibility study prior to the campaign had been conducted. The study report recommended a lead gift of $2 million or more to launch the campaign and provide a base for the rest of the campaign. The Bishop said to me, "I've never asked anyone for a million dollars before let alone two million dollars. I'm in your hands, Jim." I told the Bishop it didn't take any more effort to ask for two million dollars than it did to ask for a million.

Since the Bishop was new to his diocese, he obviously did not want to fail in his attempt to secure a lead gift for the campaign. In addition, he did not want to embarrass himself with the lead gift prospect. He certainly did not want to be rejected outright by the prospect. It was a tense situation to say the least. The fact that the prospect was a hard-nosed businessman, who was not adverse to speaking his mind, even to his own Bishop, did not make the matter any easier. The pressure was on, because the Bishop knew from my counsel that the only person this prospect would respond to was "the Bishop" himself.

I told the Bishop that, "The worst thing that could happen is that the prospect could say 'no'." If that happened, he should not take it personally. The campaign was more important than his personal feelings of rejection. He agreed.

As for being embarrassed, I told the Bishop that I could not imagine any situation in which he would not be able to handle himself despite his lack of experience in soliciting gifts. In effect, I was saying to him, "You didn't get this far by being a slouch."

In terms of his fear of failure, I told him I would take responsibility for the failure of this solicitation since the size of the gift was predicated on my research. I would not encourage him to make such a solicitation if I did not believe he had a better than fifty-fifty chance of obtaining the gift. (This Bishop would not have blamed me or anyone else if he had not gotten the lead gift. He was too gracious to do that. However, he did take some comfort in knowing that he could point to poor advice from his consultant if he did fail.)

My suggested strategy was for the Bishop to have three meetings with this prospect. The first meeting was to get acquainted; after all, the Bishop was new to the job and the community. In the second meeting he would discuss the capital fund drive. During the third meeting he would elicit a response. Otherwise, he would "close" the prospect. The Bishop was not too thrilled with such a cold and calculating fund raising strategy.

The Bishop's first meeting with the prospect was a dinner meeting at the prospect's home. The Bishop had offered to take the prospect to dinner, but the prospect insisted that the Bishop come to his home. The prospect was very much in charge of this first meeting. He was using the occasion to size up the Bishop: What kind of Bishop would he be? Would he be a leader? Did he just want money? Fortunately, the Bishop passed the test. The prospect was most impressed with his new Bishop. The stage was now set for the next meeting.

The second meeting took place at the Bishop's home where he reciprocated by providing dinner. After the usual amenities, the Bishop got right to the point by mentioning the capital campaign. He told the prospect how important it was to establish momentum for the campaign with a lead contribution in the $2 million range. He stated his case as I had suggested in a briefing paper, but with his own "spin" on each point. What happened next nearly floored the Bishop. The prospect simply said, "I'll do it, Bishop."

The prospect had made up his mind that he would take a lead role in the campaign, but preferred to cover the details of his gift in a later meeting as he wished to return to discussing a wide range of church issues with his Bishop. In short, the prospect was enjoying his special "audience."

The third meeting never took place. The Bishop believed that the best way to handle the details of the $2 million gift was to reduce the prospect's offer to writing. So the Bishop's assistant and I prepared a letter from the Bishop to the prospect, recalling the offer to contribute the $2 million, but leaving the terms to the prospect. The prospect responded with a $100,000 payment and the promise of another $1,000,000 in the same year and said this pattern of payments would continue for "an indefinite period." The Bishop got much more than he asked for and said to me, "Got any more people you want me to call on?" His fears had been overcome.

The fear of reciprocity isn't so much a fear, but rather a consequence of having obtained a major gift from a friend or business associate. Every campaign I have ever been associated with has had its share of reciprocal gifts. In other words, the solicitor elects to approach a particular prospect, knowing full well that a $10,000 gift can be obtained; however, the solicitor will have to make a similar contribution to the prospect's favorite charity. This happens often in the YMCA, Boy Scouts, Girl Scouts or similar youth agencies in which the children of board members are involved. If faced with a reciprocal situation, offer to consider the request at a later date. By all means, don't discuss it during your ask.

Knowing how to solicit a major gift is the key to overcoming the fear of asking for it.

Fear vs. Asking Point/Counterpoint

Point	Counterpoint
"I hate to ask for money."	People like and expect to be asked.
"I'm afraid to ask."	People give because they're asked.
"Asking is demanding something from someone."	Ask with a question.
"If I ask I may hear 'No'."	Ask and you may receive. Don't ask and you won't receive.
"It hurts to ask; it's too stressful."	Not asking hurts those you aim to serve.

© James A. Donovan

CONSIDER THE PROSPECT'S NEEDS

When preparing to ask for major gifts, it's important to understand the prospect's needs. To illustrate this aspect of the asking process, we turn to the noted psychologist Abraham Maslow, famous for his hierarchy of needs. His research tells us that humans have six basic needs ranging from the need to eat to the need for optimal fulfillment.

A brief review of Maslow's hierarchy of needs is an important lesson in understanding the prospect. Maslow says that human beings have certain needs in the areas of biological demands, safety, love, esteem, freedom and fulfillment. We all need food; we need to feel safe from harm; we need companionship; we all want to feel good about ourselves; we desire the freedom to do what we want; and, ultimately, we desire total fulfillment - to live and experience life to the fullest.

The pinnacle of this hierarchy, fulfillment, is most important to the major gift prospect. These are people who have accomplished most of their goals in life except one, giving back or creating a lasting legacy. An example of such a person is Ross Perot. He has accumulated vast wealth. I would venture a guess that he sought the presidency of the United States out of a desire to be more fulfilled as a person. As president, he could have made a difference in a way he has not been able to as a businessman. He is also the ideal major gift prospect. Creating visions or legacies, and making a difference with his own money are obviously goals important to his sense of ultimate fulfillment.

The lesson to be learned from Maslow is that you must appeal to a person's sense of fulfillment. **Show them how their major gift can and will make a difference in their own life first and in the lives of thousands of others for generations to come.**

Understanding the Prospect's Needs

The Prospect Wants To:

❏ Have his/her interest addressed.

❏ Do what is right.

❏ Make a proportionate gift.

❏ Look good to peers.

❏ Participate in a win/win proposition.

❏ Pay the gift on his/her terms.

© James A. Donovan

WHO ARE THE BEST PROSPECTS?

Your best major gift prospects are usually right under your nose. They are your regular contributors, those who are already actively supporting your institution, organization, or agency. On the other hand, if you are just starting out, then your best prospects may be contributors to a nonprofit organization similar to yours.

Major gift solicitation must be approached like archery. You draw the bow and aim the arrow not merely at the target, but at the bull's eye - dead center. You should carefully target your major gift prospects by considering the center of the target as a pool of individual prospects, such as directors of the board. Outside that tight circle are other individual prospects, such as prior donors, then corporations, foundations and others.

To properly prepare for a major gifts campaign, you must take inventory, prepare the master list of prospects, and then evaluate each prospect's ability to give. Resist the temptation to just go out and get some money. Instead **prepare**, then go out and get the money.

Analyzing your current donor base and prospect list is an important first step in identifying major gift prospects. You will notice a pattern of giving and various cutoff points in levels of giving. Most people give at the beginning, middle, or the end of a particular range. By analyzing the pattern of giving by your donors, you can then categorize gift levels in ranges such as $5,000 to $9,999; $10,000 to $25,000 and upward. A donor's past history or the evaluation of a prospect's potential will determine at which level the donor or prospect should be included. Most fund raising campaigns are conducted according to dollar amount, as opposed to classification of donors or prospects, such as businesses, foundations, or professional associations. This places emphasis on the amount of the gift rather than the origin or source of the gift.

Consider screening the entire database of donors electronically with a vendor such as **Donovan Management's eZScreen** that can append to each *individual* name important information such as the donor's age, household income, income producing assets, net worth and home market value.

```
Age ............................................................................55
Wealth Indicators
Household Income ..................................... $120,000
Income producing assets ........................... $450,000
Net worth ................................................ $2,500,000
Home market value .................................... $500,000
```

For each wealth indicator a score of 1 to 5 is given with 5 being the highest score. If a prospect got a score of 5 on each of the four wealth indicators above, his score would be a perfect 20. All names with scores of 17-20 are put in the A Group, those with scores of 14-16 in the B Group and remaining scores in the C Group. You now have segmented the database by ability to give, but not inclination to give. For that you must dig deeper with advanced research on a customized basis, either through a vendor like Donovan Management or your in-house prospect researcher.

The most helpful advanced research is social information on the prospect. What clubs or organizations does he belong to? Hobbies, interests, awards received, speeches given, religious affiliation, political party are all helpful. **In the end you must find the prospect's passion in life.** From there you show how that passion matches your mission.

But first, do the math to determine the number of prospects you need. You must have a major gifts table which shows how many gifts are required at each of these levels in order to achieve your total goal.

For example, if you are trying to raise $1 million in major gifts, a typical gift table would resemble the table below.

A TYPICAL GIFT TABLE $1,000,000

# Prospects	# Gifts		Range		Cumulative
3	1	at	$200,000	=	$200,000
6	2	at	$100,000	=	$400,000
12	4	at	$50,000	=	$600,000
60	20	at	$10,000	=	$800,000
120	40	at	$5,000	=	$1,000,000

Notice that each of the five levels of gifts needed to reach the goal represents twenty percent of the total goal. You can also have a gift table based on a ten percent factor; that is, each of ten levels of giving would represent ten percent of your total goal. It all depends upon your goal, the number of prospects in your prospect pool, and at what level each prospect has been evaluated.

As a general rule, the number of prospects vs. actual gifts needed in the gift table should be a ratio of three to one. Not every one you solicit is going to give at the level requested, nor is everyone going to commit to a gift. Therefore, don't launch your major gift program until you have three prospects for each gift required at each level to meet your goal.

SUMMARY OF PART I.

1. Know your statistics and recognize that over eighty-five percent of the billions of dollars contributed each year in the United States is given by individuals - your best market for major gifts.

2. The reason so many more people haven't become major gift donors is because they haven't been asked.

3. The primary reason people give, next to being asked, is because of their religious beliefs and out of a sense of helping others, not for tax purposes.

4. Volunteers and staff are afraid to ask because they don't know how to ask.

5. Appeal to the major gift prospect's sense of personal fulfillment. Go beyond the usual successes in life.

6. Your best prospects are people who are already supporting your organization or one that is similar. Research their ability to give.

7. Develop a gifts table, then prepare a comprehensive prospect list, evaluate it, and make it conform to the requirements of the gift table.

8. Don't launch your major gifts program until you have three prospects for each gift required to meet your goal.

NOTES:

NOTES:

***By failing to prepare,
you are preparing to fail.***

- Benjamin Franklin

Part II.

WHERE TO BEGIN

Begin at the top. In major gift fund raising staff is on tap and volunteer leaders are on top. Why? Because *people give money to people* they know/trust and see that they are giving freely of their time to a cause, not to staff who are paid for their time. Peer level, *volunteer driven capital campaigns* are always the most successful. Thus, there is no substitute for volunteer leadership that leads by example and is passionate about the mission of the organization.

The role of volunteer leadership is:

1. To enlist others to serve on the campaign cabinet or on a committee such as a Special Gifts Committee.

2. To assist in identifying and rating potential donors to the campaign, particularly at the $10,000 level and up.

3. To assist in educating and cultivating the prospects before they are asked to give to the campaign.

4. To encourage leadership gifts consistent with their commitment to the campaign and their personal ability to give; in other words, not a token gift but a major gift.

5. To give careful thought to who is the best person to solicit prospects and to devise an asking strategy that is to the benefit of the donor first and your

organization second. This includes tax savings for giving as well as special naming opportunities in recognition for their gift or in honor or memory of a loved one.

6. To prepare leadership for making solicitations by being fully informed or trained by a consultant in major gifts before you make the ask.

7. To attend campaign cabinet meetings and be actively involved in all discussions, ask questions, stay positive and keep the campaign on track.

8. To have the discipline to follow the campaign plan and timeline and to avoid taking shortcuts. By taking shortcuts, you end up short of your goal.

9. To communicate with campaign staff and fund raising counsel as often as necessary when preparing for meetings, cultivation events or solicitations. You can't be over prepared.

10. To not promise a donor anything that must be approved by the full board of directors beforehand, such as the naming of a building and/or a space or place in it or on the grounds.

11. To inform prospective donors of the Donor Bill of Rights.

The Donor Bill of Rights*

*The following is from the
Association of Fundraising Professionals, Alexandria, VA*

Philanthropy is based on voluntary action for the common good. It is a tradition of giving and sharing that is primary to the quality of life. To ensure that philanthropy merits the respect and trust of the general public, and that donors and prospective donors can have full confidence in the nonprofit organizations and causes they are asked to support, we declare that all donors have these rights:

I. To be informed of the organization's mission, of the way the organization intends to use donated resources, and of its capacity to use donations effectively for their intended purposes.

II. To be informed of the identity of those serving on the organization's governing board, and to expect the board to exercise prudent judgment in its stewardship responsibilities.

III. To have access to the organization's most recent financial statements.

IV. To be assured their gifts will be used for the purposes for which they were given.

V. To receive appropriate acknowledgement and recognition.

VI. To be assured that information about their donation is handled with respect and with confidentiality to the extent provided by law.

VII. To expect that all relationships with individuals representing organizations of interest to the donor will be professional in nature.

VIII. To be informed whether those seeking donations are volunteers, employees of the organization or hired solicitors.

IX. To have the opportunity for their names to be deleted from mailing lists that an organization may intend to share.

X. To feel free to ask questions when making a donation and to receive prompt, truthful and forthright answers.

*Copyright 2008, Association of Fundraising Professionals (AFP), all rights reserved. Reprinted with permission.

HOW TO SOLICIT YOUR BOARD OR CAMPAIGN COMMITTEE

Premise: Those who give birth to great causes do so by leading the way. When it comes to asking others to support the cause, a prerequisite is that those leading it ought to have provided the first gifts of the campaign, thus the term leadership giving. It sets the example for others to follow.

Formula: Anyone in a leadership position is expected to make a gift that will be one of his/her top three gifts to charity for the year the campaign takes place. The gift should also be in proportion to one's financial ability to give. In other words, not a token gift.

Objectives of Campaign Giving:

1. 100% participation

2. 100% proportionate giving (meaning according to one's financial ability to do so) by all leaders involved

3. Collective board/committee giving equals a respectable percent of the overall campaign goal, usually 5% or more

Process:

1. Chair or Co-Chairs of the board or Campaign Committee announce the giving objectives and rationale. Allow time for leaders to "think about" their gift.

2. Chair or Co-Chair make their gift/pledge in writing and report it to the CEO.

3. Chair and Co-Chair challenge key committee chairs to do likewise.

4. Key committee chairs challenge their committee members to do likewise.

Timetable:

One month from start to finish.

Benefits of Meeting Giving Objectives:

1. Provides fund raising momentum for the campaign and the first opportunity to report campaign progress in newsletters and email updates.

2. Satisfies requirements of grant making foundations about how much the leadership has given.

3. Strengthens the case for giving when leaders ask others to give as they have done so themselves.

4. Makes stakeholders out of all leaders involved, providing a vested interest in the success of the campaign.

5 Demonstrates to prospective donors leadership's commitment and strong belief in the mission of the organization.

Confidentiality and Recognition:

- Gift amounts are kept confidential unless donors wish for their gift to be known by allowing their name to be listed in the honor roll of donors used in campaign materials or the donor desires a naming opportunity. The campaign pledge letter has a place to indicate the donor's preference.

- Only the aggregate of board giving is made known to the full board and public and the percent of participation.

- A donor can be listed anonymously in the honor roll if so desired under a particular giving category such as Leadership Gifts $100,000 or more or even on a room plaque, simply by listing the donor as Anonymous.

- 90% of all donors do seek recognition as they want others to know they believe in the mission.

- Of the 10% of donors who say they want to remain anonymous, 90% of them, for the good of the campaign, can often be persuaded otherwise as their name attracts other donors.

HOW DO WE FIND POTENTIAL DONORS

- Keep in mind the best prospects are donors currently giving to your organization. Yes, right under your nose. They will give again. Just ask them.

- Then, ask them to give you the names of their friends, their holiday mailing list, their Rolodex or Blackberry list of contacts and vendors.

- Check out honor roll listings in the annual reports of other nonprofit organizations for active donors, particularly at donor club levels such as Founders, President's Club, etc.

- Check out walls of honor in lobbies of hospitals, colleges, museums that list donors to building campaigns.

- Check out donors to other causes/institutions.

- Check out names of buildings, street names (these are often named after founding families in a town or village).

- Most importantly, check out the Internet and worldwide web. Prospecting there for prospective donors has never been easier. Most nonprofits list their donors by level of giving.

- Check out the yellow pages of businesses.

- Check out lists published in business magazines that show CEO compensation levels.

- Check out the **Foundation Center** listing of private or family foundations.

HOW DO WE RATE/EVALUATE PROSPECTS

Prospect Rating and Evaluation Methodology

Objectives: To identify three (3) prospects for every gift needed
To identify a potential gift code for each prospect
To identify the prospect's area of interest (if possible)
To identify the best person to solicit the prospect

Types of Gifts Needed:		**Code**
Pacesetting Gifts	$500,000 +	PG
Leadership Gifts	$100,000 to $499,999	LG
Major Gifts	$25,000 to $99,999	MG
Special Gifts	$10,000 to $24,999	SG
General Gifts	$3,000 to $9,999	GG
Other	Under $3,000	O

Range of Gifts	# Gifts Needed	Received	# Prospects Needed
$500,000+			
$100,000+			
$25,000+			
$10,000+			
Under $10,000			

Prospect Rating and Evaluation Methodology

Standards of Giving for $35,000,000
Major Gifts Campaign

From 2005-06 to 2010-11

Note: Based on 3:1 ratio of major gift prospects to donors

# Prospects	# Gifts	Size	Cumulative	Percent
Leadership Gifts				
3	1	$7,000,000=$7m	$7,000,000	
6	2	$3,500,000=$7m	$14,000,000	
12	4	$1,000,000=$4m	$18,000,000	51%
Major Gifts				
30	10	$500,000=$5m	$23,000,000	
60	20	$250,000=$5m	$28,000,000	
120	40	$100,000=$4m	$32,000,000	91%
Special Gifts				
60	20	$50,000=$1m	$33,000,000	
120	40	$25,000=$1m	$34,000,000	
300	100	$10,000=$1m	$35,000,000	100%

© James A. Donovan

Sample Inventory/Checklist

Key Information Needed on each Major Gift Prospect

Info Needed	Completed	Incomplete
Area of interest	x	
Giving history		x
Largest ever gift		x
Best person to get appointment		x
Best team to solicit	x	
Ask amount	x	
Offer of recognition/place space		x
Friends of prospect who have given		x
Anticipated objections		x
Plan B if first ask results in "maybe"		x
Practice the ask		x

Be sure you have an X in the completed column on <u>all</u> key information before making the ask.

© James A. Donovan

Sample Prospect Research Form
Charity USA

Name   **Contact Info**   **Rating Code**   **Comments**

1.

2.

3.

4.

5.

6.

7.

8.

9.

10.

Submitted by:_____

SAMPLE

Job Description for Prospect Researcher

The Prospect Researcher will be responsible for the daily operation of prospect research, including prospect identification, compilation of qualification data, initial analysis of prospect information, and prospect management. As a member of the fund raising team, this position will provide support to the fund raising staff by researching new prospect sources, responding to prospect leads and providing prospect evaluation data and profiles. The Prospect Researcher takes primary responsibilities in managing the organization's database for storing the research findings and maintaining the integrity and confidentiality of prospect data.

Qualifications

Bachelor's degree in Library Science preferred. Must have some knowledge of standard and online reference/information sources; should be able to read and interpret financial, technical, and trade documents, and journals, including annual reports, real property files, and court records. Ability to write and edit logical and detailed reports in clear and concise manner is vital.

Experience with fund raising software, such as (note preference), personal computers in a "Windows" environment, computer logic concepts, and online systems. Must be able to work under pressure to meet deadlines; must be able to analyze and prioritize assignments; also must judge the amount of time to spend for the expected outcome, according to the importance of a project and the type of information needed. Must be highly organized, analytical, accurate and detail oriented. Strong interpersonal skills preferred.

Duties & Responsibilities

1. Proactively identify potential prospects.

2. Acquire and analyze financial and interest data about individuals, corporations and foundations that are potential prospects for major gifts and grants to the institution.

3. Prepare comprehensive biographical and financial profiles on all types of prospects in a succinct and useful format as needed by fund raising staff and volunteers. Work with fund raisers to incorporate strategy into research reports.

4. Establish and maintain Moves Management (Prospect Management) system within the database to track prospect cultivation process. Provide various reports for the Executive Director for prospect management and analysis.

5. Serve on the Moves Management Team, possibly as facilitator.

6. Provide leadership assistance to the Director of Advancement Services in acquiring various prospect research tools by researching and evaluating the resources. Also act as a liaison to such vendors.

7. Create and maintain Prospect Research Policy & Procedures in order to maintain the integrity and confidentiality of prospect information.

8. Provide training and technical assistance to fund raising staff in use of a software database in the scope of prospect research.

9. Work on special research projects as assigned by the Director of Advancement Services.

SUMMARY OF PART II.

1. Begin at the top – volunteers on top, staff on tap. Fund raising must be volunteer driven and staff supported.

2. Adhere to the *Donor Bill of Rights*.

3. Begin with the internal "family" first – your board and staff. Encourage/challenge them to give *in proportion* to their ability to do so and in keeping with their passion for the mission of your organization.

4. The best prospects for major gifts are right under your nose -- donors that are already giving. Focus on them before attempting major gift prospects with little or no connection to your organization.

5. Make sure you have at least three prospects for each gift you need on the campaign gift table. The last thing you want to do is run out of prospects. If you do, your campaign is sure to fail.

6. Use the Internet to augment research on prospects. However, keep in mind the best way to research and evaluate a prospect's ability to give is with peer review. Keep your campaign volunteer committee focused on this on-going process.

NOTES:

NOTES:

Part III.

THE ASKING PROCESS: THE APOC METHOD

> **Money is not given, it has to be raised.**
> **Money is not offered, it has to be asked for.**
> **Money does not come in, it must be gone after.**
>
> Anonymous

The key to obtaining major gifts is asking for them. People who have the ability to make major gifts to your institution expect to be asked in a manner that is clear, concise, and convincing. **Better yet, turn the ask into an invitation to become a part of your institution's exciting mission by inviting them to make a difference.**

There are only three ways to ask for money. You can send for it through the mail, call for it on the telephone, or request it in person. **When it comes to obtaining a gift of $10,000 or more, whether it be a cash gift, a stock gift or a deferred gift, such as a unitrust, the most effective way to do it is face-to-face.** When planning the major gifts campaign, you should avoid the temptation to write letters, send email proposals and use the telephone. Few people have the clout to request a major gift by mail or phone. A gift of $10,000 or more (whether cash or deferred) is a significant sum of money. It's a serious gift and requesting it should be taken seriously.

PREPARATION

Before you ask for the major gift, you should develop a profile of the prospect. The more you know about the prospect's prior giving, fields of interest, circle of friends, impressions of your institution, personal frame of reference, and potential objections to giving, the better prepared you will be. As noted earlier, information on each of these subjects is vital in profiling the prospect.

The main sources of information about your donors are in your own development office files. Simply check the donor's prior giving record to determine the history of giving, the amount of the most recent gift, the cumulative amount given, and the purpose of the gift.

Another way to identify major gift prospects is through a Feasibility Study. It's called that because it tests whether it's feasible or not to attempt to raise a certain amount of money in major gifts for what is considered a capital campaign, usually for bricks and mortar or endowments. Participants in the study are asked if they would give to an institution's proposed campaign and, if so, in what approximate range --- $10,000-$25,000, $50,000-$100,000. The participants are then asked by the consultant conducting the study, "Whom do you know who could give in these ranges if properly motivated?" The study uncovers the names of potential major gift donors to which your consultant can direct you.

There are any number of ways to obtain information on prospects that you didn't find in the files. Start with your current donors and board. Ask them if they can evaluate the prospect's ability to give, his or her areas of interest, and circle of friends.

Always cultivate a relationship with the prospect before asking for the major gift. Allow sufficient time to involve prospects in the activities of your institution. The old adage, "Friend raising before fund raising" should be heeded.

The following is a suggested checklist of questions in developing a profile for each major gift prospect:

QUESTIONS TO HELP DEVELOP PROSPECT'S PROFILE

	Yes	No
• Has the prospect contributed to your organization in the past?	❏	❏
• Is the prospect a new prospect?	❏	❏
• Is the prospect a current donor you want to upgrade?	❏	❏
• Have you asked other major gift donors or board members if they know the prospect?	❏	❏
• Have you run a wealth analysis (screening) of the prospect to determine his/her capacity to give?	❏	❏
• Is the prospect a major donor to another nonprofit organization in your community?	❏	❏
• Is the prospect involved in your organization and if so in what capacity?	❏	❏
• Has the prospect been consistently cultivated by being invited to and attending special activities or events during the year?	❏	❏
• What have you learned about the prospect from doing online research? (i.e., accomplishments in business or professional life, hobbies, political ties, religious involvement, sports or family life).	❏	❏
• Who advises the prospect in terms of his banking, financial or legal affairs?	❏	❏

Use caution when approaching financial or legal professionals as they will not and should not give you confidential information about prospective donors. My approach to them is this, "I am thinking about approaching Mr. O'Malley for a major gift to our capital campaign, but I don't want to embarrass myself, my institution or Mr. O'Malley by asking him for something he is not capable of doing. Is he, in your opinion, a good candidate for a major gift to our campaign?" Note: You haven't asked the banker, lawyer, or accountant to reveal anything specific about their client, but rather to give you a green light, red light, or caution light before approaching the prospect.

Many a solicitation has failed right from the start because the prospect's prior giving was not acknowledged. Find out if the prospect has given to your institution in the past, how much was given, and for what purpose. If proper acknowledgement was not given, then make sure that it is before you proceed any further. Knowing the prospect's personal interests can help you in establishing rapport. When you and the prospect have a mutual interest, such as fishing, jogging, or collecting antiques, you can get to know each other by discussing these topics.

You've heard the expression, "Birds of a feather flock together." Knowing the prospect's friends can be a great help, especially if one or more of those friends has already contributed to your campaign.

What is your general understanding of the prospect's impressions of your institution, organization, or agency? Positive, negative, or somewhere in between?

Does the prospect have a personal frame of reference such as having experienced a downturn in business due to a recession, the high-tech boom/bust of the late nineties, the hardships of the Great Depression, or other dramatic incidents? These may be clues as to how the prospect thinks about, manages and gives his money.

What objections do you anticipate that the prospect might raise?

THE APPOINTMENT

Getting the appointment is vital, for without it you don't get the opportunity to ask for the major gift. Keep in mind that the larger the major gift request, the more appointments that may be needed. A request for $1 million or more may take two or three appointments with the prospect. The first to inform the prospect about the goals and aspirations of your campaign. The second to suggest a range of participation, and the final appointment to ask for the gift. The number of appointments should be carefully thought out ahead of time. Each prospect is different.

The best way to get the appointment is for a current major gift donor to call and ask for it on behalf of himself as the assigned solicitor. Regardless of who makes the call - you or a current donor - let the prospect know up front that the reason for the appointment is to ultimately discuss a major gift. But you should let the prospect know that, for now, the meeting is only to provide him with information and explore his possible participation. Then give two dates and times and ask which the prospect prefers. Try to meet Tuesday, Wednesday, or Thursday as the beginning of the week and end of the week are generally not convenient. **When making the appointment, use this opportunity to set the tone for the upcoming meeting. Let the prospect know that you are excited about what you are trying to accomplish on behalf of your institution.** For example, the current donor or whoever calls for the appointment could say to the prospect:

"Mr. Anderson, I am a member of the campaign team, which is working to build a cancer center next to our local hospital. As you know, our community hospital is a first-rate facility. We will soon be able to offer cancer patients the quality of service they receive from the regional hospital 100 miles north of us. Patients won't have to endure that four-hour drive each week."

"The campaign is off to a good start, and I was hoping you would allow me the opportunity to personally tell you about the impact this new cancer center will have on our community and those it serves. I am available at a time convenient for you."

Once you get the appointment, send a letter confirming it or an email reminder. The advantage of regular mail is you can send other documents you want the prospect to review prior to your appointment. It may also end up in the hands of his assistant so now two people in the same office know about the appointment.

STRATEGY

Now that you have the appointment, you should use the time prior to your actual visit with the prospect to prepare the strategy you will employ when requesting the major gift. **Your strategy should begin with a decision to use one solicitor or to double team the prospect.** I strongly suggest double teaming. A solo solicitor is fine, provided he has total confidence in his ability to answer all the tough questions that might arise and to persuade the prospect to give. Solo soliciting works best when the request is a relatively sure thing.

When double teaming, try to use a peer-level major gift donor, that is, a donor who has given at the level you are requesting and a key staff person of your institution. Use the volunteer to lead off the conversation and introduce the subject of the visit. The staff person should then set the tone by telling the prospect how the fund raising campaign has serious implications for the long-term viability of your institution.

Have the peer-level donor describe the project to be funded and ask for the gift. The staff person should gently reinforce the volunteer's "ask" by restating the long-term implications and fielding any tough objections. Finally, the volunteer should be prepared to close by asking whether or not the prospect will agree to the major gift request.

Six Point Checklist For Double Teaming

Use a staff member with a peer-level volunteer to use the Double Teaming method.

	Professional Staff	Peer-Level Volunteer
Who Leads?		X
Who sets the tone?	X	
Who describes?		X
Who asks?		X
Who reinforces?	X	
Who closes?		X

© James A. Donovan

Utilizing this strategy during your visit will enable you to conduct your solicitation in a concise, professional, and courteous manner. You want to leave the prospect with the feeling that this was the best solicitation ever experienced.

THE APOC METHOD

There are four essential elements in the Asking Process itself. We call this **APOC**. Just memorize these letters and you will remind yourself of these four essential elements: **A** for amenities, **P** for presentation of the case, **O** for objections, and **C** for closing. Here are the components of the **APOC method**.

Amenities

The day has arrived for your appointment. What you do in the first five minutes of your meeting is critically important. This is the amenities phase of your visit; when done right, this phase can set the tone for the entire meeting.

1. **Start out by warming up the prospect with a sincere compliment.** Make sure it's sincere and not contrived or else it may backfire.

2. **Get the prospect talking about personal interests and passions.** Not only will it make the prospect comfortable, you will probably pick up some information that you can use later in your presentation.

Prepare yourself mentally to perform the amenities and follow these simple suggestions. It will make your job a lot easier and make you more comfortable.

Preparing for amenities means having the discipline to engage in this important aspect of the solicitation. It's simply a mental commitment you make much like the effort you make when trying to remember the name of someone you have just met. The amenities are often an overlooked aspect of relationships. Once you are engaged in the amenities, you discover all kinds of clues about the prospect's interests. This is valuable information, which allows you to set a relaxed and informal atmosphere for the remainder of your appointment.

Presentation of the Case

Nothing will make or break your request for a major gift more than how the prospect views your case for support. Follow the three C's formula for presenting your case: be clear, concise, and convincing. The presentation of your case should be a concise five-minute live presentation which addresses the questions below. (Also, see sample Talking Points Exhibits section.)

ANSWER THESE QUESTIONS ABOUT YOUR INSTITUTION

- Where has your institution been? Its past.
- Where is your institution today? Its present status.
- Where does your institution want to go? Its future aspirations.
- What financial investment of philanthropy is needed to reach your destination? In short, the fund raising goal.

Live, DVD, or PowerPoint?

Nothing is more forceful or impressive than a "live," rational presentation of the case for support. When you present the case with a combination of logic and emotion the case begins to sell itself. Resist the temptation to rely on a DVD or PowerPoint presentation to make your case. State your case in person with passion, then use visuals and sound to reinforce it at the end of your appointment with the prospect. But remember, you must tell the story, make the case, as it can be told/stated only by you.

If you must use a DVD, another option is to make it a "leave behind." Now the prospect can view it privately. Remember, we all think of DVDs and PowerPoints as a source of entertainment. Your visit with the prospect is not to entertain, but to inform and convince the prospect to contribute to your campaign. Therefore, make your case in person and let the visuals reinforce/entertain later.

Likewise, resist the temptation to rely on your fund raising brochure to explain your case for support. This document, like the DVD, contains your case, but it, too, is a "leave behind" reinforcement tool.

The DVD's main advantage is that, unlike a human narrator, it won't forget a key point. Increasingly, major gift campaign directors are using a combination of verbal and video presentations. You should seek the advice of your fund raising counsel to weigh the merits of your situation prior to using videotaped presentations.

The presentation of your case should cover the questions as noted earlier. To introduce the subject of the case for support, I recommend to clients that they begin by saying to the prospect:

"Obviously, your time, Clifford, is valuable, so I'll get right to the subject at hand. I want to tell you where our institution has been, where it is today, and where we hope it will be in the future, as well as the investment it will take to reach our destination."

Then you can lead into the presentation of your case, for example:

"Clifford, you have been a sustaining contributor to the Children's Discovery Museum for the past five years. You know the value of private support. The museum has come a long way since it was founded by Dr. Walters right after World War II. He provided the land and that old warehouse. At the time we thought, 'Who would ever drive that far out

of town to visit a country museum?' With the growth of the community, we are now centrally located. We have four main buildings - three exhibit buildings and the main office complex. As you know, General Electric, IBM, and NationsBank have provided major sponsorship of these three exhibit halls over the past forty years. The museum has had millions of visitors. It has also been recognized by the Smithsonian in Washington as one of the southeast's best children's museums.

Presently, we have reached a plateau. We either maintain the status quo or push on and develop new high-tech interactive learning exhibits that educators tell us are much more effective as teaching and learning tools than stand-alone exhibits. The board of directors and museum staff have done extensive research, and we believe we have a solid plan for the future. It's called Discovering The 21st Century, a futuristic exhibition that is on the cutting edge of computer, video, and interactive technology. In fact, we even have plans to share these exhibits via satellite hookup with smaller museums around the country. This is an exciting and bold step for us. It will cost $5 million over a period of three years to build this new exhibit hall and another $2.5 million for a maintenance endowment, for a $7.5 million total. When completed, our museum will be more than a great children's museum. It will be an economic contributor to our local economy.

This is all great, Clifford; however, I'm sure nothing compares to seeing the expressions on the faces of the children when they discover the joy of learning. Think how your son, Mark, would react in this stimulating environment."

Notice that this presentation answered all of the questions noted earlier. It told him where the institution has been, where it is today, where it wants to go in the future and the investment cost to get there. That is how you present your case for support, by taking the prospect on this journey with you of where you have been, where you are, and where you want to go.

Asking for the Major Gift

Key Words and Phrases

Given the previous (support/new interest) in (name of project), I was hoping you would join with (names of peers giving at the same level) in helping us meet our ($ amount) goal. We would be most grateful if you would consider a major gift in the range of ($ amount) payable over three years.

© James A. Donovan

Having said this, you must now ask for the gift. Here's the best way to state the request:

Summary of Key Words and Phrases
When Asking an Active Donor for a Major Gift

- In the past, you have been a most generous donor to our organization.
- The campaign is off to a good start. We have raised a third of our goal already.
- The campaign is a major gifts effort, not be confused with the annual giving program.
- When this campaign is successful, it will enable our organization to…
- I hope you will consider a gift in the range of $….
- Can you think of any reason why you can't make this gift?

Stating the Key Words and Phrases

In the past you have been most generous to our institution. Your gifts have funded a dozen scholarships here at Prep School USA. As you know, the Campaign to Endow Prep School USA is underway. We are seeking a total of $25 million to secure the school's financial future. When fully funded, the endowment will provide even more scholarships and annual budget support.

The campaign is a major gifts effort. This means we are seeking relatively large (major) gifts from a small number of donors in phases. Pledges are spread over three years, longer if needed. The campaign's lead gift of $5,000,000 came from your classmate George Smith, class of 1950. His gift represents 20% of the campaign goal.

Presently the leadership gifts phase of the campaign is underway. This phase seeks gifts of $1,000,000 or more and it's off to a good start. We need a total of five gifts in this range and right now we have four.

As an alumnus of Prep School USA and given your devotion to her, I was hoping you would consider being that final $1,000,000 donor. By doing so, we can close out the leadership gifts phase and begin the special gifts phase.

More importantly it will give the campaign tremendous momentum by putting us at 40% of the campaign goal. I am here to formally invite you to be a part of the Endow Prep School USA. But before you respond, let me say two final things:

First, on behalf of the board of directors of our institution we are most grateful for all you have done over the years for the school. And second, I have made my own gift already and due to my circumstances it's a stretch gift for me but by no means at the level I am asking you for today.

Can you think of any reason why you can't make this gift to your alma mater?

Having stated the request (and a great closing statement) you must become as silent as a rock. It's the prospect's turn to talk, ask questions, or raise objections. And, it's your job to listen and respond. See the Sample at the back of this book for an example of a personalized donor proposal. (Take the time to make it look professional and personal.)

Here is a second example of how you could state your case for a hospital:

I am sure that the Mother Superior for these Irish Sisters never dreamed that the six-bed medical clinic they founded over 100 years ago would have grown into a hospital holding company and ownership of six hospitals in three mid-Western states. What a testimony to vision, hard work, and stewardship of resources over the decades. Today, we have the best hospital in the region. With the completion of our expansion program, we will also have the best equipped and staffed emergency treatment facility.

This hospital started with its original mission of providing medical care to injured railroad workers back in the 1890's. Now it has come full circle again by building a state-of-the-art emergency trauma center, the only one of its kind in a 500-mile radius.

As the leading hospital in our region with 450 beds and a reputation for outstanding quality care, we believe we are well positioned to obtain support for this next phase of our expansion, which the people of our city and region need and deserve.

The number of emergency cases at the hospital has increased thirty percent each year for the last three years. This is due to a corresponding population increase in the metropolitan area itself, which grew by ten percent from 2000 to 2005. The local industrial development commission is predicting a five percent population growth between now and 2010.

Since most of the emergency treatments involve industrial accidents, many of the region's top major employers – International Harvester, Ford, and Dupont – have agreed to take a leadership role in the fund drive. Between them, they have pledged the first twenty-five percent of the $5 million campaign goal or $1,250,000. An additional $1 million has been pledged by Mrs. McCowan, the wife of the late John C. McCowan, founder and president of Union Bank. We think this is an excellent start, and we are now concentrating on contributions in the $500,000 range. We will need two gifts in this range to develop a large base for the campaign before taking it to the general public.

Our fund raising feasibility study indicated that unless we raise approximately $3 million in fewer than six gifts as a base from which to launch the campaign, then we would have a difficult time convincing the community at large to support the drive. Unlike our capital drive ten years ago in which our largest gift was $400,000 with hundreds of small gifts from

Asking For The Gift

- ❏ Acknowledge the prospect's prior giving, if any.

- ❏ Express hope that the prospect will be supportive of your goals.

- ❏ Drop names of the prospect's peers who have already given gifts.

- ❏ State the amount of gift or range of the gift.

- ❏ Be silent. Use silence to get a reaction.

- ❏ Leave a written proposal as a record of your request.

© James A. Donovan

our door-to-door efforts, this campaign will require a few, but substantial gifts.

Most people know that they will spend some time in a hospital, but few believe they will ever end up in an emergency room due to an accident or sudden illness. This emergency room is for people who are facing a real sense of urgency. So, too, is our campaign. If we can complete the campaign by December 31 of this year, we can take advantage of low construction costs and declining interest rates. Now is the time to do this.

I've talked long enough. I'd like to hear your thoughts on this exciting project. How do you feel about it?

By concluding your case presentation with such an open-ended question, you give the prospect the opportunity to express his or her convictions and you avoid being too presumptuous.

To become fully proficient in stating your case and asking, complete the following exercise.

CASE STATEMENT EXERCISE

1. **Write your case and rewrite it until you have it as concise as possible and it flows naturally.**

2. **As you write, keep in mind that you are writing something to be said out loud, not read by the prospect. There is a difference.**

3. **Write as if you were speaking to the prospect.**

4. **Read it aloud and tape it. Play the tape.**

5. **Then edit it again.**

6. **As you reread it out loud or listen to the tape, ask yourself again if it flows.**

7. **Is it clear, concise, and convincing?**

How To Analyze Your Donor Base

Conduct A Three-Year Analysis of Giving

	Individual	Corporations	Foundations	Special	TOTAL
Year $					
Year $					
Year $					

© James A. Donovan

Last Year's Analysis of Giving

Range	Number of Donors	Amount
$1 - $49		
$50 - $99		
$100 - $249		
$250 - $499		
$500 - $999		
$1,000 - $2,499		
$2,500 - $4,999		
$5,000 - $9,999		
$10,000 - $24,999		
$25,000 and over		
TOTAL		

© James A. Donovan

Analysis of Giving and Prospect Identification

Range	Number of Actives	Number of Prospects	Total Actives and Prospects
under $100			
$100 - $499			
$500 - $999			
$1,000 - $2,499			
$2,500 - $4,999			
$5,000 and over			

© James A. Donovan

Analysis of Giving Last Year

Various Categories	Number of Donors/Prospects	Percentage of Converts
Actives[1]		100%
Lybunts[2]		50%
Sybunts[3]		30%
Inactives[4]		20%
Prospects[5]		10%
Suspects[6]		5%

1. Actives refers to those who donate yearly to your organization.
2. Lybunts are those who gave last year, but did not give this year.
3. Sybunts are those who gave in past years, but did not give this year.
4. Inactives have never given to your organization, but are associated in some way with your organization.
5. Prospects are good sources to ask for donations
6. Suspects are those on whom more research must be conducted to determine if they are good prospects.

© James A. Donovan

Analysis of Giving By Actives

Annual Giving	Number of Donors	Percentage to Upgrade*
$1 - 49	1,500	
$50 - $99	600	
$100 - $249	400	50%
$250 - $499	200	50%
$500 - $999	100	50%
	Area of Opportunity**	
$1,000 - $2,499	75	25%
$2,500 - $4,999	50	25%
$5,000 - $9,999	25	25%
$10,000 - $24,999	10	10%
$25,000 over	5	10%
TOTAL		

* Percentage to Upgrade refers to the number of donors who are possibly candidates for giving at a higher level to your organization.

**Area of Opportunity is a guideline by which you determine what percentage or number of major donors you will ask to upgrade.

© James A. Donovan

SUMMARY OF PART III.

1. The more prospects you ask for major gifts, the more funds you will raise.

2. Know your prospects before you ask them for a major gift.

3. Don't overlook amenities. Present your case live; don't rely on a video tape.

4. Use the key words and phrases shown in the example given when asking for the amount of the gift.

NOTES:

*When I'm getting ready to reason with a man,
I spend one-third of my time thinking about myself
and what I am going to say,
and two-thirds of my time thinking about him
and what he is going to say.*

- Abraham Lincoln

Part IV.

DEALING WITH OBJECTIONS

Over the years that I have given my seminar on major gifts, participants have told me that the method dealing with objections has been the most valued aspect. Like the seminar participant, you will find the special exercise in this section as a great way to begin. Knowing how to respond to objections in the right way will make all the difference as to whether or not you get the major gift. You, your professional staff, and volunteer solicitors have heard the common objections to giving to their institution, organization, or agency. Some of the more generic objections which apply to a cross section of nonprofits are as follows:

"You spend too much money on administration and fund raising."
"Your agency just duplicates the work of other agencies."
"Why ask me for money? Why don't you ask a local foundation?"
"Your goal is too high for this project; you haven't done your homework."
"This is not the time for asking: the economy is bad."

These are real objections, or so they seem. At least they are real to the prospect. As such, they must be dealt with, not overlooked or made light of. To do so would be a serious mistake. **Objections provide you with one of the best opportunities to score points, to persuade the prospect with facts, and overcome these roadblocks to giving.** You should **welcome** objections, not fear them. When properly handled, objections can be turned into motivations for giving.

Complete the Inventory of Objections exercise on page 80. Start by listing, as they come to mind, the most common objections to giving to your organization. List as many as there are. Consult with other volunteers and staff. Ask them to do likewise, then prepare a master list of objections.

Once the master list is completed, go back and create a new list of the most frequently raised objections. Start with the one objection mentioned most often and proceed to the one least mentioned. Now you have a better understanding of what obstacles to expect when talking with your major gift prospect.

This exercise works best when you have a small group of solicitors and staff who make up your major gifts team. Convene them, and ask them to perform this exercise. Then give everyone the opportunity to come up with an appropriate answer to each objection. Once the group is satisfied with the quality of the answers, publish and circulate this list of objections to your team. They will feel much more confident in asking for a major gift knowing that they have anticipated objections and that they are prepared to deal with them.

FIVE STEPS TO HANDLING OBJECTIONS

These are five steps you need to keep in mind when handling objections:

STEP ONE
Acknowledge them as they arise. Don't overlook them, or you will be sending a message to the prospect that you are not concerned about his feelings. Do that and you lay the groundwork for a sure decline to your major gift request. When you acknowledge the objection, you communicate to the prospect that you are listening.

STEP TWO

Don't debate with the prospect. Arguing creates a negative atmosphere and pits the prospect against you. Instead, educate the prospect by providing facts he or she may not be aware of as answers to the objections. Most people are willing to change their position, provided they are given the facts that allow them to do so.

For example, if a prospect says, "This state university doesn't need to be raising private funds. The state provides more than enough funds to run the university from my state tax dollars. So why is the university trying to raise $10 million?"

You need to reply with the facts. For instance, you could respond with the following:

"First of all, less than forty-five percent of the state university budget is provided by the state. That shocked me, too, Mr. Smith. Another fifty percent comes in the form of federal grants, auxiliary services (such as book sales, food, vending machines and seminars), tuition, and financial aid. Only five percent of the budget comes from private contributions. Thus, you might ask why does such a small percentage of funds make such a big difference? Let me illustrate: we pay an average salary of $85,000 to a full-tenured professor. Most private colleges would pay the same professor $10,000 more. If we want to compete for the best professors (and I might add we have some of the very best), then we must try to close this gap. The only way we can close the gap is to raise private funds because the state will only provide the basic salary, not any incentives or upgrades.

"The same is true for the library. Our library budget was cut by the state last year and the year before due to state revenue shortfalls. This year we are asking for a thirty percent increase in the library budget just to get back to where we were two years ago. That's not growth, that's maintaining the status quo. Private support provides us with the discretionary dollars to acquire new library books and periodicals.

"In short, state funding provides for the essentials. Private funds enable us to upgrade quality at all levels when funding is stagnant."

STEP THREE
Correcting erroneous information is the fastest way to diffuse an objection. For example, a prospect says to the solicitor, "I know that your fund raising expenses are running at twenty-five percent." And you counter by saying, "That was true two years ago, but as our new audited financial statements point out, they are now running fifteen percent and our goal is to reduce them to twelve percent next year."

STEP FOUR
Get back to the subject at hand (the prospect's gift) once the objection has been satisfied. There are a lot of detours on the road to reaching the prospect's heart. Resist the temptation to stray from the path. Stay on the right road and continue your journey. For instance, you could bring the conversation back around to the gift with the following statement: "As I was saying, private support is the key to maintaining and providing quality. I know you share my concern for quality as it is widely known that your own company is a quality-driven organization."

STEP FIVE
Maintain a common ground with the prospect. Stress the things you have in common, not those that you differ on. The example of how much you are spending to raise funds could be strengthened by saying, "I am in total agreement with you on keeping our costs down." Also, maintain a common ground on the areas of mutual interest, such as quality, excellence, keeping costs down, value for your dollar, outstanding teachers or doctors or museum pieces. The common ground issues should come from information you picked up about the prospect at earlier meetings. You should be able to bring these back into the conversation if you have listened carefully to the prospect.

In dealing with objections, be sure to use the Three F's formula: "I feel, I found, I felt." It goes like this:

"Clifford, I feel the same way you do about keeping our fund raising costs down. In fact, I found myself asking the same questions two years ago when I was reading the annual report and financial statements. Like you, I felt it was time to take some action, and I did."

This formula is a powerful relationship builder. It makes it clear that you are listening and responding with great empathy.

When handling objections, heed this sage advice from Abraham Lincoln:

"When I'm getting ready to reason with a man, I spend one-third of my time thinking about myself and what I am going to say, and two-thirds of my time thinking about him and what he is going to say."

For example, allocate one-third of the time to answer the objection to your response and two-thirds of the time for continued listening to the prospect's reaction to your response. This way, you won't appear to be defensive in responding to the objection.

Inventory of Objections

List the most common objections for not giving to your organization.

1. _____ 5. _____
2. _____ 6. _____
3. _____ 7. _____
4. _____ 8. _____

Describe the best response to overcome each of the objections above.

1. _____ 5. _____
2. _____ 6. _____
3. _____ 7. _____
4. _____ 8. _____

Be ready to "educate" your prospect even if your prospect has given to your organization in the past.

© James A. Donovan

SUMMARY OF PART IV.

1. Complete an inventory of all possible objections to giving before asking.

2. Always acknowledge the prospect's objections. Never overlook the objections.

3. Don't debate or argue with the prospect; educate him instead.

4. Use facts to convince the prospect of your point of view.

5. Once you have answered the objections satisfactorily, get back to your request.

6. Provide yourself, and all other solicitors with a master list of objections and responses to them.

7. Use the Three F's Formula to build rapport with the prospect: "I feel, I felt and I found."

NOTES:

NOTES:

*We make a living by what we get,
but we make a life
by what we give.*

- Winston Churchill

Part V.

HOW TO CLOSE THE MAJOR GIFT

Legend has it that the late Henry Ford was confronted one day by his golfing partner with whom he had been playing for several years. His partner said, "Henry, I've been playing golf and talking business with you for five years now. Why haven't you ever given me a chance to manage the company's insurance program?" To which Mr. Ford replied, "Because you never asked."

In the business world, asking a customer for their business is the first order of business. Equally important is knowing how and when to be **direct** about it. In sales, they describe this as "the close." Closing a major gift request or the sale of insurance involves the same basic techniques. **The "asker" must make the effort to clearly and specifically elicit an answer to his or her request.** Here are three special closing techniques which you can use.

THE NO / YES CLOSE

Have you ever noticed how people generally like to say "no" to requests for almost anything? Children with their parents, "Mom, will you extend my curfew by an hour?" Parents, "No." Wife, "Honey, let's start an exercise routine this summer by walking three miles together." Husband's response, "No thanks." Or in business, "Boss, how about a raise?" Boss, "You're kidding, right?" We have become programmed to say "no" to telephone solicitations, street vendors, and door-to-door salespeople.

On the other hand, the word "no" can mean "yes." By using the no/yes close, you allow your prospect to say "no," but when he does he ends up responding affirmatively to your request. It's not a trick, but rather a combination of a clarifying question and a close at the same time. Here's how it works.

"Clifford, we have used enough of your time. We have described for you why we think our institution needs and deserves your support. In the process, we have answered some objections you have raised. Can you think of any reason why you shouldn't honor our request for a major gift in the range of $75,000?"

When asked this way, the prospect can only respond in one of two ways: He can say "No, I can't," which means "yes" to the request; or "Yes, I can." Then he proceeds to bring up an objection that was hidden, giving you the opportunity to deal with it.

When the response is, "Yes, I can think of a reason why I shouldn't give," answer the objection by using the techniques noted earlier for dealing with objections. Then restate your request like this: "Now, Clifford, is there any reason why you can't see your way clear to making this gift?"

We suggest you practice this closing tactic with friends, family, and business associates prior to using it on a major gift prospect. For example, when talking to your boss you might say, "Can you think of any reason why I shouldn't be given the added responsibility for our company's newest client?" You will be amazed at how this politely aggressive and direct way of asking can get you what you want - an affirmative response to your request.

THE INVESTMENT CLOSE

The next best closer is the investment close. This is used with those prospects who are stringing you along, the person with whom you have met three or four times, and keeps asking you for more information and more time to make a decision. In each case, your instincts tell you that the prospect is putting you off and hasn't got the nerve to tell you "no." The investment close puts pressure on the prospect and is a reminder that your major gifts campaign is serious business. **In a polite but firm way, you're telling the prospect, it's now or never.** No more coming back. No more long-winded philosophical discussions. For example, you might say the following:

"**Clifford, we have invested considerable time and resources in this campaign and our four meetings with you. We do have a deadline for completion of this campaign - December of this year. It's now October, and our best estimate is that we have sufficient cash flow, which will allow us to break ground on the museum's new exhibit hall by February of next year. As a businessman, I know you understand our urgency to begin construction before interest rates go back up. Can we count on you today for your gift of $75,000 or more?"**

With this closing technique, you have conveyed to the prospect that you are no longer going to let him stall or put you off without a definite answer one way or another. You have also given him a sound business reason as to why you want an answer now, a reason he should understand as a businessperson - higher interest rates. Surely, you run the risk of a "no" answer, but you also make it clear that you are going to move on to other prospects and keep your campaign on track. You can always go back to this prospect later, but at least for now you have stopped wasting your time and kept the campaign on schedule.

THE EGO CLOSE

The third closing technique, the Ego Close, is the oldest one in fund raising. It goes like this:

"**Clifford, you are one of the most influential people in our community. What you do causes other people to follow your example. The museum's campaign for a new exhibit hall stands to attract many of your friends and colleagues once you have made your gift. Can we count on you to contribute in the range of $75,000?**"

You must be selective in the use of the Ego Close. If the person you use it on is not a "Mr., Mrs., or Ms. Big" of the community, it will surely backfire. On the other hand, appealing to a person's ego is important and even expected in major gift campaigns. People like to be flattered, especially when they know they are truly powerful and influential.

THE DOUBLE-IT TACTIC

Having explained these three closing techniques, I wish to offer a tactic that may enable you to double the amount of money you have just obtained. Once a person agrees to a major gift, don't miss the best opportunity you have to get another one of equal size. Employ the Double-It Tactic. This tactic is a bold step in the major gift solicitation process. It must be handled with finesse. It's only used **after** the prospect has enthusiastically agreed to a major gift. Here's how it works:

"**Clifford, your commitment to give $75,000 to the museum campaign is very generous and much appreciated. However, how about doubling it?**" **Pause for effect.**

Then very quickly interject that you don't mean for Clifford to raise his gift to $150,000, but rather help in the campaign by agreeing to solicit a $75,000 gift from one of the prospects on your list that he knows. If he agrees and is successful, then he has doubled his contribution to the museum.

There is no better time to sign up a donor as a major gift solicitor than right after he has contributed his own gift. Discipline yourself, your staff, and your volunteers to use the Double-It Tactic. Not only does it provide you with more major gifts, but also an expanded team of solicitors.

The Double-It Tactic

Use this tactic to double the gift after the pledge is made.

- Acknowledge the gift and express your gratitude.

- Tell the prospect that more gifts in this amount are needed to meet the goal.

- Ask if the donor would like to double his or her gift.

- Pause for a reaction. Then explain that you are not asking him or her for more money.

- Explain the benefits of the donor calling on others who are his peers.

- Provide the donor with a list of names.

- Get a commitment from him or her to solicit gifts.

> Don't be afraid to try this technique. There is no better time to do so.

© James A. Donovan

FOLLOW-UP

Many a major gift has been lost for the lack of proper follow-up after the request. Always write a personal note expressing thanks to the prospect. Thank him or her for taking the time to meet with you, then confirm what the prospect agreed to. This shows that you listened and that you are being thorough as well as professional about the major gifts campaign. Use this occasion to send additional information, answering questions that may have been asked during your meeting. Most importantly, stress the deadline for the first payment on the pledge and the impact this payment has on the project's cash flow. Be gracious, appreciative, and complimentary.

The Follow-Up

Promptly send the prospect a letter following your presentation. In the Follow-Up Letter include these features:

❏ Thank him or her for taking the time to hear the presentation.

❏ Express the hope that the prospect will make payments on his/her pledge by a specific date.

❏ Offer to answer any further questions that the prospect might have.

❏ Stress the deadline for completion of the drive or campaign.

❏ Remind the prospect of the urgency of your program or project.

© James A. Donovan

SUMMARY OF PART V.

1. People prefer to say "no" and that "no" can mean "yes" to a request when the request is properly stated.

2. Don't waste time and resources on procrastinators. Push for an answer.

3. Appeal to the ego of the powerful and influential leaders who expect such flattery.

4. Double your money and volunteer work force by using the Double-It Tactic.

5. Follow up with prospects by sending a letter of acknowledgement and thanks.

A CHECKLIST OF REMINDERS WHEN ASKING FOR THE MAJOR GIFT

- 1. Be a good listener as well as presenter.

- 2. Be your own charming self.

- 3. Ask for a gift in a particular range and ask for enough.

- 4. Remain positive throughout the entire meeting with the prospect.

- 5. Make sure that you and other solicitors have made your own gifts before soliciting someone else.

- 6. Know your prospect and do your homework before asking.

- 7. Tailor your presentation to the donor's interests.

- 8. Anticipate the prospect's objections and be prepared with answers.

- 9. Leave a written proposal as a record of your request.

- 10. Use knowledge to reduce the fear of asking for major gifts.

NOTES:

Frequently Asked Questions About Major Gift Fund Raising

Over the years, I've presented seminars dozens of times based on the information included in this book. During the seminars, participants have asked me many of the same questions. As expected, much has changed in philanthropy since the first printing of this book. The more recent and new questions that have been popping up are listed below, along with the responses.

1. **Google and other search engines make prospect research fairly easy today. If one needs more information on a prospect he can hire firms like yours to do more in-depth research. How ethical is this?**

   The information we obtain is all in the public domain. That means it's either self-reported by the prospect, reported/stored by a government entity like the Securities and Exchange Commission for publicly traded stock, or it's information compiled, by vendors who sell it to firms like ours. For example, we can find a person's age because our vendor pays to access drivers license information state by state. And each license has the driver's date of birth. This is important when the person is 62 years of age or older and eligible for Social Security. It also means the prospect may be more inclined to make a bequest or deferred gift, given his age and fixed income, than an outright gift.

   As for the ethics, the Association of Professional Researchers for Advancement (APRA) Statement of Ethics says, "Advancement researchers must balance an individual's right to privacy with the needs of their institutions to collect, analyze, record, maintain, use and disseminate information. This balance is not always easy to maintain." In short, researchers are expected to do their job without bias, in confidence, with accuracy, according to clear internal policies for storage and access of information, with honesty as to the truthfulness of the information obtained, and without any conflicting interests by the researcher.

2. **Can you suggest other sources on the ethics of asking for major gifts?**

In 1996, I wrote a review of the book, *The Ethics of Asking: Dilemmas in Higher Education Fund Raising* that was edited by Deni Elliott, Mansfield Professor of Ethics and Public Affairs and professor of philosophy at the University of Montana. The review was for *Metropolitan Universities: An International Forum,* a higher education quarterly. In that review I wrote, "This book is a must-read for all nonprofit fund raisers, not just those in higher education. It should be placed on the shelf right next to the Bible." Believe me, the book is that good.

3. **Finding wealth information on prospects is fairly easy. How important is asset and income information when asking for a major gift?**

Surely, you need to know if the prospect has the financial capacity to make the gift in the range you are asking in, for example, $25,000 or $50,000. After that, knowing the person's passions in life are most important. That kind of information is harder to get. That's why I say there is no substitute for the old fashioned peer level prospect rating and evaluation sessions where volunteers, current donors, and staff, sit around a table to review the list and provide insights such as the prospect's hobbies, interests and passions. Never assume a high powered executive tough guy doesn't like cats. Look at Ernest Hemingway.

4. **Many authors and consultants have lists such as the five worst mistakes when fund raising. What would you consider the most common mistakes major gift fund raisers make?**

Without a doubt, number one is taking shortcuts. I tell them if they take shortcuts they will come up short on their goal. Major gift fund raising is a systematic process that involves many steps before, during and after the ask is made. The second mistake is failure to identify prospects from the inside outward. Who among your board and current donors can make major gifts? Why does everyone want to run out and solicit the newest wealthiest entrepreneur who has no connection whatsoever to your organization? The third mistake is spending too much time analyzing the prospect's wealth at the expense of finding vital social information, such as his passions in life that have a connection to your mission. My dad was a U.S. Marine in World War II and a devout Catholic. If you were with the Marine Corps or the Catholic Church, Catholic Charities or the Catholic Missions you'd have a great chance of getting a gift from him. You wouldn't believe how many people over the years thought because he was a N.Y. State Senator he would be for dozens of causes near and dear to his district. He was, that's why he worked so hard to get State dollars.

5. **What's different today about volunteer leadership and board members relative to major gift fund raising?**

Expectations of staff responsible for major gift fund raising are way out of line by volunteer leaders and board members. Too many of them see fund raising as a retail exchange, not a philanthropic proposition. By this I mean, they think by giving staff a few credit cards and country club memberships, staff will constantly wine and dine prospects and bring in the gifts. We know, all of us in this profession, that the most successful major gift fund raising programs are those that are volunteer peer-level driven and staff supported. Sure the staff play a part in the ask. However, nothing works better than a volunteer (non-paid) solicitor making the ask. Remember, philanthropy is voluntary action for the common good. Not paid action. Staff is on tap, not on top.

6. **Those of us that represent smaller nonprofits, not the major colleges, universities or hospitals that typically get the majority of larger gifts in their community, struggle in that we often find ourselves going after the same donors. That being the case, what can we do differently?**

   First, realize there is plenty of money for everyone. Admittedly there is a pool of active, regular donors in every community. The same names keep popping up on the lists of honor rolls. However, what about the hundreds or thousands of un-invited potential donors out there? They represent millions of dollars in gifts waiting to be asked for. That's where research comes in, for example, monitoring the right business publications and social/society section of the local newspaper or weeklies.

7. **In your experience, what would you say are the expectations of the major gift prospect when being asked for a major gift?**

   To be tactfully and tastefully sought out, informed and approached. In the dozens of campaign feasibility studies we do each year, we hear from major donors that they are often put off by the tactless and tasteless way they were last asked for a major gift by the client organization or another organization they gave to. The informality of it all is a big problem for most donors. The most common complaint I hear is, "They came here and essentially assumed I would give and never really told their story, i.e., made their case. It was like, 'What can we put you down for?'"

8. **The process of major gift solicitation you suggest requires more than one visit with the major gift prospect. How many appointments are needed?**

   Depending upon the magnitude of your request, three visits may be necessary. I recommend that the first visit be a "take their temperature" session, whereby the upcoming project or campaign is discussed in general terms along with the gifts required to meet the goal. In effect, you are saying to the prospect: we are confident that if we go forward we will attract the necessary gifts needed to complete the gift table. Then you are pausing for their reaction. At this point, they will tell you whether or not they will be involved.

The second visit is the "mutual self-interest" visit where you describe the prospect's interests and how they correspond to your campaign project list. You ask the prospect to consider participating in the campaign in the giving range in which you have evaluated him/her. But let them know that they don't have to be prepared "today" to make a commitment. (This is not to say you won't take a commitment at this time, but rather send the signal that you aren't pressuring the prospect for a quick answer.) You then agree on a third meeting when you do expect to hear their answer.

The third visit is the most important. That's the one where you "close" the prospect with one of the three closing techniques described in this book.

9. **How do you go about getting an appointment with a prospect?**

The person who arranges the appointment may not be the person doing the asking. The best person to ask the prospect for the appointment is the person to whom the prospect cannot say "no". This should be a person of considerable influence, someone who may very well have no connection to your campaign, but believes that your prospect will give if properly approached. Very often, just getting the appointment means you have a better than fifty-fifty chance of obtaining a gift. Thus, the appointment maker is as important as the solicitor. By doing a little homework, you can find out who the best person is to ask for the appointment. Check around with your volunteers and other major gift donors. They'll know who the best person is for the assignment.

10. **We have a limited donor base. How can we find more major gift prospects?**

There really isn't a shortage of major gift prospects or information about them. In fact, the information you need is usually in your database. If not, check the annual reports of other nonprofit organizations or institutions in your city. These reports contain the names of potential major gift prospects.

Annual business reports are another good source of information as they list the names of corporate officers and their salaries. You can also contract with a prospect research company. Many of the national fund raising firms now offer prospect research services. Just wandering around town can also be a beneficial exercise. There are several listings of donors in the lobbies of hospitals, civic buildings, churches, museums, and libraries.

11. **You recommend asking for a gift in a range rather than a specific amount. This goes against conventional wisdom. Why do you prefer the range approach?**

For one simple reason: People like to challenge themselves. They are just as likely to respond to a challenge from themselves as from someone else. By giving the prospect room to move, you are allowing them to find their giving comfort level. This will backfire on you if the gift amount you need doesn't equal the minimum amount you are requesting. If you must have a $100,000 gift, ask the prospect to consider a gift in the range of $150,000. Always ask for more than the actual amount the prospect was evaluated for since most evaluations are on the conservative side.

12. **In our community, it seems that the same people are always being called on to make major gifts. How can we avoid this?**

Don't avoid it, but do your best to make a clear distinction between your cause and the other causes you know the donor is supporting. People don't mind being asked, but they do mind being taken for granted. Remember: major gift donors are often looking for new opportunities for giving.

13. **Who is better at asking for a major gift? The staff member who knows the institution or a board member who may know the prospect on a personal basis?**

    Both are important and both should be used in the solicitation. Teaming up is the best way to approach a major gift prospect.

14. **How much should be spent on providing donor recognition devices?**

    No more than is necessary, but enough to show the donor that he/she is appreciated. The best judges of this are the donors themselves. This is the one area where I strongly recommend that the donors decide upon the level and the cost of recognition along with staff input.

15. **Volunteers think they know how to ask for money and resist training seminars like ones you present or even special ones in conjunction with capital campaigns. What advice do you have for encouraging volunteers to participate in major gift training programs?**

    Don't call it training. Describe it as orientation or an executive briefing. Keep it to a couple of hours and bring in an outsider as a facilitator. Be sure to include a lot of humor. Historically, these sessions have been too cut and dry. That's why people don't like them. This should be an occasion to put the fun back in fund raising. Cover the points noted in this book, but set up your agenda to allow for some storytelling and testimonials from veteran solicitors. Tell your volunteers that the most successful campaigns are those which follow time-tested principles of fund raising. When presented in this manner, volunteers believe it is important to go with a proven methodology.

16. **Of all the points you cover in your major gift training programs, which one is the most important?**

    Preparing ahead of time. My counsel to clients is to be committed to the process of preparation. If you are not willing to prepare yourself in the techniques of major gift solicitation, then you are wasting your time and building failure from the start. You must resist the temptation to run out and "get some money." An outstanding major gift campaign takes both preparation and discipline.

17. **What impact does the economy have on major gift fund raising and the future of nonprofit organizations?**

    There is always a silver lining in every economy. While some folks are hurting, others are making money. Remember: during any downturn in the economy or a recession, some sectors gain, some lose. After the September 11, 2001 terrorist attacks on the U.S., the airlines and other travel related industries suffered major financial losses. On the other hand, software firms dealing with airport security made huge strides by filling a need nationwide. The greatest impediment to raising money in a poor economy is dealing with naysayers. Once they dominate the discussion, enthusiasm for raising major gifts dwindles fast. Keep a positive attitude regardless of what the forecasters tell you.

    The future of nonprofit organizations depends on how they are managed. The management of nonprofits is what is under scrutiny today.

    We are going to see more mergers of nonprofits, many going out of business for lack of support, and the continued proliferation of causes, such as the environment. Pressure for merging will come from local foundations and businesses that expect a certain economy of scale.

Why have five local agencies helping the homeless when one will do? I believe hospital fund raising is in for tough times as we approach guaranteed health care for all.

As for the availability of money in the future, I believe it's always there for the asking, unless, of course, we experience a true depression. The problem is that most fund raisers are seeking contributions from the same sources and the same commonly known donors. It's like the Gold Rush – everyone gravitates toward the mine that hit a vein and the next guy wants to tap into it. Fund raisers do the same thing. I think that the real potential for giving lies with the entrepreneurs that we read about in major business publications like Business Week, Forbes, Fortune, Inc. Magazine and local weekly business journals. That's where the reports are made on businessmen and businesswomen who are quietly working hard to create wealth. They maintain a low community profile and hustle seven days a week. Then they get bought out, retire early or start up another company. To me, these people are a great source of potential new money available for the asking. To get to it will require extensive prospect research and patience.

Basically, fund raisers are too busy chasing after annual fund dollars. I wish foundations would provide more grants for staffing development offices, especially in the area of prospect research. It seems to make more sense (and cents) to give money where money will be leveraged as opposed to giving out matching funds or one-time program grants. I've noticed that some foundation executives in the last few years have warmed up to the idea of funding development operations. Hopefully, more will do so in the future.

18. **What are some of the tough questions that prospective donors ask and how have you answered?**

There are two tough questions major gift prospects regularly ask me. The first is about the Chief Executive Officer of the institution or organization.

Just like a stockholder in a company, prospective donors want to know about the top management of the company in which they are buying stock. I'm constantly asked to objectively evaluate and rate a CEO in terms of his or her leadership ability, management competence, commitment to the institution, and integrity. This is not to say that if a CEO doesn't get an "A" on each criteria that a major gift will not be forthcoming. The prospect is simply looking to confirm his or her own suspicions about the CEO. They expect an outside independent consultant like myself to be able to give them an objective evaluation of the CEO. And I do.

The other question is always financial. Does the organization exercise good stewardship of the contributions they have received? Are the funds properly invested to obtain the maximum return? Has the organization received a qualified audit in the last three years? These are all good questions, which should be asked. These questions are more important than ever today. Since the United Way of America scandal, several trade publications and major newspapers have published investigative feature stories on the subject of salaries of nonprofit executives, the percentage of funds actually going to the people the organization says it serves, and the cost of raising funds.

19. **What personality traits are most important in the fund raising profession?**

To survive in this profession you have to have a personality that is gracious. You also need to have a generous spirit, be socially astute (better listener than talker), and possess a sense of humor, tact, and the ability to hang loose and not get too serious about things. And, of course, you must be professionally competent to begin with.

20. **How have the techniques for raising funds changed over the years? What has caused those changes?**

The biggest change I have seen over the years is the push for major gifts. It seems like everyone now wants to go after major gifts. Deferred giving was the thing to push for years ago. Today, it's a combination major/deferred gift. But the big change has come in who is soliciting the major gifts. More and more, the staff of nonprofit organizations is doing the soliciting. There is a decline in what we call volunteer peer-level major gift solicitation. In the seminars I have conducted on this subject in the last five years, I am amazed at the number of professional staff people who tell me they are being pressured to perform this function. This is a disturbing trend. As a professional, I know that there is no substitute for peer-level solicitation. Apparently, a growing number of volunteers today are unwilling or don't know how to solicit major gifts. That's why I wrote this book and travel around the country doing so many seminars on this subject. Volunteers and staff need more confidence in asking for major gifts. Too many are afraid of asking. I can't believe I'm spending so much time convincing and training volunteers and staff alike to get back to and become comfortable with traditional peer-level solicitation.

21. Are the newly affluent different as opposed to those who are the established wealthy?

There's a real difference in terms of giving, time and money. The old wealth seems to give more money and less of their time. The newly affluent get more involved in an agency also by volunteering their time.

22. If a meeting with a prospective donor is going poorly, what do you do? Describe the ways in which a meeting can go astray or awry.

I have been in solicitations that went astray. It's nerve-racking because you know you are losing ground with the prospect. After a couple of attempts to get things back on course, I usually bring the meeting to a head by saying, "You obviously have some serious concerns which we must address and which we are not prepared to answer today.

However, by next week at this time, I'll have the answers you want." Then I ask the prospect to meet within a week or sooner. The longer you stray, the weaker your case gets. I learned a long time ago that I can only bail out so much water in my boat when someone is shooting it full of holes. There comes a time to stop rowing and a time to plug the holes.

23. How do you know when it is time to quit pitching and leave?

There is a great line in the movie Glengarry Glen Ross about closing. Alex Baldwin tells his salesmen to Always Be Closing - the ABC method. When you get a gift commitment, acknowledge it immediately by thanking the prospect. Don't, like a lot of solicitors do, keep on rowing your boat. I remember a solicitor who kept talking while the donor was trying to complete and sign the pledge card. The donor got so distracted by the solicitor's ramblings that he actually put the card aside and uttered to the solicitor those horrible words, "I'll mail it in."

24. What changes do you foresee in the next several years for fund raisers?

- For those wanting a great career and a well paying job the future is very bright because so many seasoned fund raisers are or have retired causing a supply shortage at a time when demand for major gift fund raisers is at an all time high. This is further complicated by the fact that many mid-level rising stars in the profession have left for the for-profit sector. These professionals have told me and other consultant colleagues that they left because their CEO and board had unrealistic expectations of them as major gift fund raisers and did not want to follow standard practices of major gift fund raising. Those who stick it out gain solid experience and can move up to well paying jobs.

- Leadership volunteers will continue to be difficult to recruit because of pressure on them to improve the corporate bottom line and because of increased work loads due to corporate restructuring. Technology is driving multi-tasking of staff so firms can employ fewer employees by making the ones they have work harder.

- Congress will insist that the IRS scrutinize nonprofits more closely.

- More capital campaigns will rely on larger lead gifts in "flooring" capital campaigns. Instead of a fifteen percent lead gift perhaps a fifty percent lead gift on a matching basis. Those that really have the capacity to give in these ranges need to be challenged like never before. There will be more competition as more and more nonprofits are created. Major gift training for volunteers will be vital.

- Winning corporate grants will require much more alignment with corporate interests.

- Individuals will continue to support those organizations they know rather than making first-time gifts to an unknown charity.

- Special events will become more important than ever in broadening the base of "friends", as it's easier to get people to participate in an event than to make a first-time outright gift.

- More institutions will expect their in-house development staff to do more on their own and rely less on outside consultants. There will be a great deal of staff burn-out due to the unrealistic expectations of boards.

- Many nonprofit boards (start-up ventures in particular) will be tempted to hire staff or consultants on a basis of percentage-of-funds raised because they don't have a sufficient budget to raise money, and they think this arrangement is a good deal for them. Beware! Both the Association of Fund Raising Professionals (AFP) and the Giving Institute of Leading Consultants to Nonprofits and other associations advise against this practice. Under AFP guidelines, staff can receive incentive compensation as a percentage of their salary, not as a percentage of funds raised.

A Final Word

As I conclude this book, I want to share my personal conviction about the importance of fund raising. I believe that raising money is one of the most noble and honorable professions there is today. Each day offers the challenge to leave this world a little better than how we found it. This philanthropic sector of our society is the one that:
- Has a bias toward those on the bottom rather than the bottom line.
- Reminds people that "a mind is a terrible thing to waste."
- Gives life to the sick and dying.
- Makes life worth living for those who suffer physical or emotional challenges.
- Instills confidence in the young.
- Prevents cruelty to animals.
- Lifts our hearts and minds to new heights through art, dance, and song.
- Gives comfort to those affected by natural disasters.
- Asks us to plant a tree instead of cutting one down.

Soon we will be raising $600 billion annually in the U.S. from individuals, corporations, foundations, and special groups to assist nonprofit entities in meeting these aspirations on behalf of our people, pets, and planet. Statistics show that there are billions of dollars more available for the asking. I believe that if we are to attract more money for the thousands of worthy and just causes in our world today, we must begin measuring generosity in America as the late Archbishop Fulton J. Sheen suggests -- *not by how much we have given, but by how much we have left over.*

Life is a constant struggle between getting and giving. When it comes to choosing one or the other, I side with Sir Winston Churchill, who said, *"We make a living by what we get, but we make a life by what we give."*

It doesn't hurt to ask for money. But, it does hurt those who need our help from voluntary giving when we don't ask. I hope this book makes it easier for you when you do ask.

SAMPLE OF PERSONAL PROPOSAL

Homeswell Retreat
CONFERENCE & CENTER

CAMPAIGN FOR HOMESWELL

The Dream Continues

THIS PROPOSAL PREPARED FOR:

Mr. & Mrs. John Anderson

SAMPLE OF PERSONAL PROPOSAL

Message from the Campaign Chairman

The "Campaign For Homeswell" is about growth, development and the future. Once again, The Dream Continues, as it must, in order to meet continuing and more demanding needs of our Diocese. Over the past few years, so many of us have been blessed with a "Homeswell Experience" of our own. The campaign we are now launching gives us the opportunity to give something back to Homeswell, to express our appreciation to the Center in an appropriate and timely manner.

In a larger sense, the opportunity to support this campaign is a vehicle to experience a new blessing. It is a gift given in the knowledge that you are contributing to the spiritual benefit of fellow Christians and others in our community, and helping the dream of Homeswell to continue.

HOMESWELL RETREAT & AND CONFERENCE CENTER
1288 RESORT TRAIL, HOMETOWN, USA 55515

SAMPLE OF PERSONAL PROPOSAL

Homeswell Retreat
CONFERENCE & CENTER

Mr. and Mrs. John Anderson
Main Street
Hometown, USA 55517

Dear John and Helen:

Your willingness to consider a major gift to this special campaign for Homeswell is very much appreciated by me personally and as a member of the campaign team. Thank you again for your interest.

As this document points out, there are some compelling reasons why this campaign must be successful. Our retreat and conference center has outgrown its present facilities. Our success has caused us to grow and has positioned us to meet the demands for the future.

There are several benefits to you personally for participating in this campaign. They are in the form of tax savings as well as public recognition of your support. This document covers both.

Please review this request with your tax advisor before making a commitment. Should you have any questions, please contact me.

Sincerely,

Jack Howe

Jack Howe
Major Gifts Chairman

HOMESWELL RETREAT & AND CONFERENCE CENTER
1288 RESORT TRAIL, HOMETOWN, USA 55515

SAMPLE OF PERSONAL PROPOSAL

[THE REQUEST]

This request, to Mr. and Mrs. John Anderson, is being made by Bishop Larry Jackson and Mr. Mark Jones on behalf of the diocese Board of Directors of the Homeswell Retreat and Conference Center for a tax-deductible investment in the range of $50,000 (over a three-year period). Your gift will be applied toward the expansion of the Center, which includes the construction of a Memorial Chapel and a new 7,400 square foot guest lodge building.

Homeswell Center has reached a critical stage in its brief seven year history. In a way, Homeswell Retreat and Conference Center is a victim of its own success. Demand for a larger more functional chapel, coupled with the need for increased overnight guest space, has limited the Center's ability to realize its fullest potential. The Board of Directors has taken an initial step toward meeting these demands by authorizing the "Campaign For Homeswell," a capital funds program designed to raise the necessary funds for this expansion. This is an active approach toward securing the funds required to move forward with Homeswell's commitment to provide a Christian environment of retreat and conference for the people of the Episcopal Diocese of Hometown, USA.

[BENEFITS TO DONOR]

In addition to realizing a tax deduction for making this contribution to the Campaign for Homeswell, the Board of Directors of Homeswell Retreat and Conference Center agrees to affix a permanent Jack and Helen Anderson plaque in the Memorial Chapel or Guest Lodge depicting appropriate words of recognition for your generous investment in the Center.

[THE CASE]

In just seven short years, Homeswell has grown from a vision to being a favorite meeting place for people of many denominations and faiths. Its many educational, human service, and community functions have touched the lives of thousands of people. The natural beauty, facilities, staff and programs offer opportunities for time away from the rigors and stress of everyday life, and for rest and relaxation, physical and spiritual renewal, recreation, study and learning, and fellowship with one another. With the addition of a full-time

SAMPLE OF PERSONAL PROPOSAL

[THE CASE] Contuned

marketing and program development person, the Center now offers an even greater variety of programs and events which appeal to a much broader audience. This increase in user demand, coupled with the projected needs of the future, has prompted Homeswell's Board of Directors to forge ahead with the "Campaign For Homeswell."

Facilities for the Future
St. Joseph Memorial Chapel (In Memory of Richard Blake)

The St. Francis Oratory, Homeswell's "sanctuary within a sanctuary," is located in the Center's Administration Building. It contains 225 square feet, and is the smallest room in this building. The Oratory serves the needs of those who wish to spend a few minutes alone in the presence of the Lord God. Its intimate design offers a peaceful place for individuals and small groups (20 or less) to pray and seek spiritual renewal and refocusing.

In addition to the present oratory, a larger more functional, multi-purpose Chapel is needed. The new Chapel will reflect Homeswell's purpose of focusing on spiritual development. Its design will allow larger groups to gather and pray in an open and spiritually refreshing atmosphere. The proposed 2,500 square foot Chapel will be ten times the size of the Oratory. It will be located just off Homeswell's entrance driveway overlooking Lake Park.

A New Guest Lodge
The present guest facility consists of two meeting rooms and 30 lodging units with the capacity for 60 overnight visitors. Guest rooms are single or double-occupancy and have freshly prepared comfortable beds and private baths.

With the addition of a new guest lodge building, capacity for overnight visitors will increase by one-third, from 60 to 90 persons. The new facility will be a single story, interior corridor building located north of the current lodging building. Also included in the new facility are separate living and meeting rooms.

The demand for the new guest lodge is a direct result of the growing number of visitors to Homeswell Center.

SAMPLE OF PERSONAL PROPOSAL

Several years ago Bishop Jackson and other Diocesan leaders had a dream of building a "special place," which would serve as a retreat and conference center for the clergy and lay people of the Richmond Diocese. Today, that dream is a reality. However, in order to continue the ministry, which Homeswell provides, it is time "to dream again."

In the words of Bishop Jackson, "Homeswell has become our special place of gathering for reconciliation, learning, relaxation and just plain fun. It is a place, which in all it is and does, proclaims the good news of Jesus Christ." The Campaign for Homeswell is designed to further enhance the growth and development of this truly "special place," and to assure that the Center continues to be an offering to the Episcopal community of Hometown and others.

Those most intimately associated with Homeswell - board members, clergy, user groups, and staff - will be invited to participate in the Campaign for Homeswell. The steering committee is chaired by Mr. Robert O'Brien. Bishop Jackson and Mr. O'Brien are just two of the distinguished individuals providing their gifts of time and resources for the Campaign for Homeswell.

[CHARTS AND ILLUSTRATIONS]

Funding Alternatives for Mr. and Mrs. Anderson

There are considerable tax savings available for an investment of this magnitude. We suggest that you consult with your accountant or financial advisor to determine the most advantageous way for funding this request over the next three years. We propose that you consider the following alternatives:

YEAR	I	II	III
Cash	$17,000	$17,000	$17,000

Securities:
Equal amounts of appreciated securities over this period. The tax deduction for a securities gift may be greater than a cash gift, provided the base is low and the current appreciation is high.

SAMPLE OF PERSONAL PROPOSAL

Assigned Interest on CDs or Trust Funds:
By assigning the interest on current CDs, the earnings can be paid to Homeswell quarterly, semi-annually, or annually, provided the payouts equal the total amount requested.

Real Estate:
A gift of real estate is also acceptable, provided Homeswell can sell the real estate in a reasonable period of time and realize a cash benefit of $50,000.

NOTE: A combination of the above methods may also be feasible. Any mutually agreeable mix of these alternatives will be enthusiastically considered by the Campaign Steering Committee.

Opportunities for Memorial Giving
The Campaign for Homeswell offers many opportunities for making gifts in memory of a loved one, living or deceased, or as a permanent testimony in your own name.

At the conclusion of the Campaign, special wall plaques will be prominently displayed in appropriate locations as a form of public recognition to donors who provide memorial gifts for the areas listed below:

New Lodging Building	$450,000
Guest Rooms (16)	$ 10,000
Living Room in New Guest Lodge	$ 20,000
Meeting Room in New Guest Lodge	$ 20,000
Meeting Room in Existing Guest Lodge	$ 20,000
Wooden Lakefront Walkway	$ 30,000
Episcopal Book Shoppe	$ 15,000
Living Room in Administration Building	$ 30,000
West Meeting Room in Administration Building	$ 50,000
Chapel Pews	$ 1,500 (each)

Any gift of $500 or more designated for the Chapel will be recognized visually in an appropriate manner.

SAMPLE OF PERSONAL PROPOSAL

[CONCLUSION[

The Campaign for Homeswell is about growth, development and the future. We invite Mr. and Mrs. Anderson to join with us in making this stage in Homeswell's evolution a successful one and to help us maintain the momentum of the past seven years. Much has been accomplished; much remains to be done. Your consideration of investing in the "Campaign for Homeswell" is greatly appreciated by us, current members of the Diocese of Hometown, and future generations of faithful people who stand to benefit from your investment and generosity for a better Homeswell Center.

Should you have any questions, please contact:

Bishop Larry Jackson
Honorary Chairman
(888) 555-3232

Mr. Robert O'Brien
Campaign Chairman
and Board Member
(888) 555-7893

Mrs. Evelyn Rochester
Executive Director
(888) 555-8483

Hank T. Harrison
Campaign Director
(888) 555-3922

SAMPLE OF PERSONAL PROPOSAL

Homeswell Retreat
CONFERENCE & CENTER

[SAMPLE LETTER of COMMITMENT]

CAMPAIGN FOR HOMESWELL

Dear Board of Directors:

This letter represents my intention to invest the total sum of $ _____ in the Campaign for Homeswell Center. This amount will be paid in (please specify) ____ cash, ____ securities or ___ other negotiable property in the following manner:

_____

_____

_____

on the following date(s): _____ for the following years: _____

It is understood that I may change or withdraw this intention if economic, health or other personal circumstances make it necessary. This (may/may not) be construed as an obligation upon my estate.

Date: _____ Signature _____

Address:
Mr. and Mrs. John Anderson
Main Street
Hometown, USA 55517

HOMESWELL RETREAT & AND CONFERENCE CENTER
1288 RESORT TRAIL, HOMETOWN, USA 55515

EXHIBITS

EXHIBITS

SAMPLE TALKING POINTS CARD

COUNCIL on AGING
Martin County

**Charles and Rae Kane Senior Center
Capital Campaign Martin County, Florida**

The Council's Past
- Started in 1974 with:
- 4 board members
- 4 staff
- 4 programs
- Budget of $45,000
- Assisted dozens of seniors
- In 2001 began long range planning process
- Hurricanes demonstrate special needs of seniors
- Council approves strategic plan for a new Center that addresses the needs of seniors during storms

The Council Today
- 33 years of service as of 2007
- 13 member board of community leaders
- 100 staff
- 24 programs
- Budget of $4.6 million
- Assists 4,200 seniors annually
- COA launches public/private campaign to raise $15 million for the Center

The Council of the Future
- A new facility to be built off Salerno Road
- Capital campaign underway with one-third of goal provided by State of Florida $5 million allocation
- Board names new facility after longtime advocates for seniors, The Charles and Rae Kane Senior Center
- Council launches a capital campaign for $10,000,000 in philanthropic gifts to achieve $15,000,000 goal

Turn card over please…

Allocation of capital campaign funds are as follows:
- $10,851,000 construction of a 33,000 foot building
- $3,000,000 endowment for building maintenance
- $500,000 campaign budget
- $649,000 contingency

Capital Campaign
- This is a campaign that seeks major gifts payable over three years. These gifts are over and above any annual gift from current donors to the Council.
- The campaign is a one time effort to raise capital dollars (brick / mortar and endowment)
- When completed seniors of Martin County will have a comprehensive facility for daily activities and services as well as a shelter from storms for seniors and their pets.

How You Can Help
- View the Kane Center at the COA website: www.coamc.org
- Request a campaign brochure, call the Campaign Office at: 772 223 7831
- Host a party of your friends so they can learn about the Kane Center
- Volunteer as a Campaign Worker
- Consider a tax-deductible gift/pledge, payable over three-years
- Consider making your gift/pledge in honor/memory of a loved one.
- Consider a gift/pledge that qualifies as a permanent naming opportunity in honor/memory of a loved one.
- Consult with your tax advisor about making a combined outright gift and Trust gift.
- Learn more about the Kane Center Campaign Office at: email.net

Used with client permission

Best Practice Tips When Asking for Major Gifts

- Remember, *it's all about the prospect*, not you or your organization. Without prospects that become donors, nothing happens. Make the prospect feel like the most important person in the universe.

- Ask *face-to-face*, never over the phone, by mail or email.

- Get in the frame of mind that you are *inviting* prospects to become part of a noble enterprise which is the fulfillment of your organization's mission

- Ask for a major gift as a TEAM consisting of the CEO, another major donor who knows the prospect or a board member. At least two people on the TEAM.

- Be *passionate* about your mission. It's about *emotion*, then logic.

- Know your case for support (your story) and tell it. Use your *Talking Points Card* as a guide. Describe your organization's past, present, future and the philanthropic investment needed to get there.

- Begin your asking with those prospects *most likely to give*. This will build your confidence for the subsequent asks.

- Ask for a gift that makes the prospect stretch. *Aim high.*

- Offer *recognition*, such as the naming of a place or space in your new or existing building or an endowed fund, in honor or in memory of a loved one.

- Answer *all* objections as they arise. Then proceed with the presentation of your case.

- Suggest non-cash (check) ways to give, such as a multi-year pledge and appreciated securities which are often more advantageous to the donor's tax situation.

- Constantly remind the prospect how he / she can *make a difference* in the life of people, pets (wildlife) or the planet.

Index

Amenities 56
APOC Method 56
Appointment 53
Closings 87
Developing prospect's profile 26
Developing your case 57-59
Donor Bill of Rights 35
Donor recognition 103
Double-it tactic 90
Double teaming 54-55
Ego close 89
Excluding the spouse 15
Fears in asking 17-22
Feasibility study 50, 100
Follow-up 14, 93
Gift table 27
Giving Statistics xi
Giving trends .... x, 6
Giving USA 6
Guilt 10
Inventory of objections 80
Inventory of the organization 5
Investment close 88
Job description for Prospect
    Researcher 44

Key sales points of the organization 5
Leadership giving 33, 36
Megagifts 12
No/Yes close 87
Obligation 10
Objections 75
Overcoming Fear 18-22
Peer-level volunteer 15, 54
Personality of solicitors 106
Preparation 50
Presentation of the case 57
Pressure 9, 10
Prospects 23, 38-39, 41-43, 51
Questions asked by donors 107
Recognition 9, 10
Religious beliefs 9, 10
Researching the prospect 26
Self-preservation 10, 11
Specific range of giving 60, 62, 64, 102
Strategy 54
Talking Points card 121
Tax savings 9, 10, 11
Three C's formula 57
Training programs 103
Video presentations 57

Other Books / Publications by the Author

50 Ways to Motivate Your Board: A Guide for Nonprofit Executives
A quick read with humor and real life stories that work. 110 pages, Second Printing: 2008

Free How-To Info / Tips / Articles / Seminar Content

Go to: www.donovanmanagement.com

Resources: Donovan Management's periodic Newsletter-- to obtain a free copy send us an email at: dmimgt@aol.com or visit our website to view Resources

Donovan's Donor Diary: http://fundraisingcorner.blogspot.com/

For information on Donovan Management publications / services / quantity discounts on book orders, please call us locally at: 407-321-0024 or 1-800-247-3023

Donovan Management, Inc.
P.O. Box 471438
Lake Monroe, FL 32747-1438

Quantity Discounts Available

Donovan Management, Inc. is a consulting firm that has been assisting organizations engaged in philanthropy since 1986. The firm provides strategic planning, management, fund raising, training and prospect research services for the full spectrum of nonprofit organizations in Florida, the Caribbean and elsewhere.

For more information on our services go to: www.donovanmanagement.com